# VISITING HOME IN POLAND AFTER 33 YEARS and WORLD WAR II TRUE STORIES

**By Fr. Marian S. Mazgaj**

McClain Printing Company
P.O. Box 403
Parsons, West Virginia 26287
1996

International Standard Book Number 0-87012-561-3
Library of Congress Catalog Card Number 96-094497
Printed in the United States of America

*Ad Majorem Dei Gloriam*
*Et Beatae Mariae Virginis*

*In Memory of My Dear Parents*
*Jozef (Bogdanski) Mazgaj*
*and Jozefa (Soja) Mazgaj*

## Contents

# Acknowledgments

I am greatly indebted to many people who in one way or another helped in the writing, correcting, and typing of the first draft and final draft of this manuscript.

In particular, I wish to express my deep gratitude to my wife, Mildred Juanita Mazgaj, for writing her diary during our travels in Poland. Without her daily account of our activities, the writing of this book would have been next to impossible.

I am also very grateful to my first cousins, Joe and Jan Mazgaj, who gave, in writing, an excellent account of the events described in the true story "He Is Still Alive". At the same time, my gratitude goes to Dr. Zbigniew Kabata, who read and corrected my description of the most unusual elimination of the Gestapo agent in Sandomierz; and to Dr. Piotr Marian Sierant for sharing with me his fine research on the crime against humanity which the Nazis committed on the inhabitants of the village of Struzki.

I would also like to acknowledge gratefully the help which I received from: Dr. John Leland, professor of English at Salem—Teikyo University in Salem, West Virginia, who read a major part of the manuscript and offered many valuable suggestions; Judy Wood, rector's secretary at St. Paul's Church, Weston, West Virginia, who typed the first draft of the manuscript; Kathy Whelan from the *Weston Democrat* newspaper in Weston, West Virginia, who typed and edited the final draft of my manuscript; George L. Bland for designing the cover and other art work in this book, and Michelle L. Mullenax, who as the editor of McClain Printing Company, worked so diligently on the final literary form of the manuscript.

# Prologue

On June 18, 1957, I visited Bishop Jan Kanty Lorek in Sandomierz and showed him my passport and visa which entitled me to leave Poland and enter the United States of America. During my visit with the bishop, I asked him for his episcopal blessing and confidentiality. The reason for confidentiality was due to the fact that the Communist authorities in Sandomierz repeatedly refused to issue me a passport. The passport which I had was granted to me by the police department in the city of Lublin, where I attended graduate school at the Catholic University. The Communist authorities in Sandomierz knew about my World War II activities and considered me a *persona non grata*. They refused to give me a passport. The bishop promised confidentiality and gave me his blessing and some names and addresses of priests in the United States of America who could be of help to me in a case of necessity.

When I kissed his episcopal ring at the end of my visit, Bishop Lorek kissed my head and wished me Godspeed. As we parted, I did not realize that we would never again see each other in this life.

The following day, I traveled to Jeziory to see my parents and my brothers and sisters. As soon as I had a chance to speak to my parents in private, I revealed my "secret" to them. On account of the young age of my brothers and sisters, I could not tell them about my intended trip to the United States.

When I said goodbye to my father and stepmother, the three of us had tears in our eyes. Due to the political conditions in Poland, we did not know whether we would be able to see each other again. As usual, I kissed my parents' hands and cheeks and we gave each other a hug. I also kissed and hugged my brothers and sisters and felt sorry that I was unable to tell them about my voyage to America.

On June 20, 1957, I boarded a train for Warsaw. During

a stop in the Skarzysko Train Station, I had enough time to visit my friends there. They were happy to see me and we took some pictures together. From Skarzysko, I traveled directly to the nation's capital. I reached Warsaw in the early afternoon and checked in at the Clergy Hotel. After refreshing myself, I went to see a lovely middle-aged couple whom I had befriended during my vacations in the Tatra Mountains. They spent World War II in England and returned to Poland in 1956.

After I said goodbye to the dear couple, I went to see my friend Jerzy Zawiejski, a famous Polish playwright who lived in the suburban part of the capital city. Since he had a great impact on my spiritual and intellectual life, I wanted to see him before leaving Poland. Unfortunately, he was not home, so I left my calling card with a short note and returned to the hotel to spend my last night in Poland before the trip to the United States.

On the following day, June 21, 1957, the weather in Warsaw was beautiful under the dark blue sky. The city was awakening to start a new day. Night vapors still hung over some sections of the city, but they were pierced by the powerful rays of the rising sun. Street cars began now to click and now to squeak as they moved from stop to stop, giving an impression that the new day was just another day. But this was not the case.

This new day was different from other days in many respects. It was a day of great solemnity. A day which contrasted so much with a normal, gray day lived by the inhabitants of the city in the shadow of the sickle and hammer and brazen slogans of Communist propaganda. A day so fresh, so colorful, so joyful, so exciting that one wished it would never end. From windows and balconies hung colorful tapestries which provided a background for displayed crosses and holy images. Apartment after apartment, house after house, block after block, street after street, all were immersed in sacred, festive mood and a spirit of anticipation.

Before the city's traffic and its noise reached its peak, the streets became empty and quiet, as if downtown life stopped for a while. All of a sudden, church bells began to peal in every part of the city, as if competing with each other and yet creating an amazing harmony of sound. At the same time, colorful processions of clergy and laity emerged from all the churches, singing hymns of faith, hope, and victory, and proceeded toward the main street, where human streams formed a great river of colorful people and banners flowing slowly but powerfully through the main artery of the capital. The city of Warsaw, the capital of oppressed Poland, celebrated the Feast of Corpus Christi under the leadership of its Primate, Cardinal Stefan Wyszynski.

The Communist puppets of the Kremlin, who by that time had exercised military and civil authority over Poland for twelve long years, felt out of place and lost in the midst of this courageous Christian city. They timidly peeked from behind the curtains of their offices and trembled in the face of the spiritual power of the river of humanity marching on the street below them and singing hosannas to Jesus Christ.

As the mighty procession was passing by where I stood on the sidewalk, I became a part of it and joined my fellow countrymen in singing hosannas to the Son of God who had chosen to visit the earthly city and dwell among men. When the procession ended, I experienced a great spiritual victory of Christ and His Church over the Communist persecutors.

A few hours later, I boarded a KLM jet en route to New York City, New York. From New York City, I flew to Buffalo, New York, where my uncle, Antoni Mazgaj and his son-in-law Andrew Celbulski, waited for me at the airport.

After ten days of warm hospitality in my uncle's home in Lackawanna, New York, I had the privilege to celebrate--for the first time in my life--the American Independence Day on July 4, 1957. A family picnic at a beach house on Lake Erie was a part of this celebration.

Following two months of vacation with my relatives in Lackawanna, my academic experiences followed one another in quick succession: Americanization School in Washington, D.C., where I studied the English Language; Cattonsville Community College, which taught me English Literature and American History; The Catholic University of America, where I earned my licentiate and doctorate in canon law and began my graduate studies in philosophy; Duquesne University in Pittsburgh, Pennsylvania, where I earned a master of arts in philosophy and completed doctoral coursework in the same field; St. John Vianney Seminary in Bloomingdale, Ohio, where I taught moral theology and canon law for ten years; the McKeesport and Fayette campuses of Penn State University, where I instructed philosophy and humanities for nine years; and finally the priestly ministry in parishes in Ohio and West Virginia.

# Part I
# Visiting Home in Poland After 33 Years

## Chapter I

The most recent dramatic changes in the Soviet Union and its satellite countries encouraged me to visit Poland, my native country, which I left as a graduate student in June 1957. In spite of the fact that I was in touch with Poland through correspondence with my relatives and friends, I had no clear idea what to expect after thirty-three years. I had some fear of visiting my native land that I had been forced to leave for political reasons.

In the afternoon on Friday, June 15, my wife Mildred Juanita Ankrom and I, along with our two teenage sons, Joseph and Marian, boarded a United States Air jet at the Pittsburgh International Airport, bound for Frankfurt A.M., Germany. I must add that this flight of U.S. Air was the company's maiden flight overseas. The president of the company, some executives,and also some stockholders were aboard the jet. The flight attendants showered the passengers with food, drinks,and useful gifts.

We landed in Frankfurt Saturday, June 16, shortly after 8:00 a.m. After claiming our luggage, we went to Avis to pick up our VW Passat, which we had reserved a week before. The car was in excellent shape and had a very large trunk to accommodate all our suitcases.

Soon, we left the city of Frankfurt and were on an excellent superhighway which led north toward Hamburg. There was no speed limit on the highway. At first we were not used to the speed with which the German drivers drove, but after a while we got accustomed to it and proceeded as fast as everybody else. It appeared to me that over sixty percent of the cars on the highway were made by the Mercedes-Benz Company.

After a few hours of driving north, we changed direction and proceeded east toward Dresden. At about 4:00 p.m., we began to look for a hotel and took an exit to Herleshausen, a town near the highway. Soon we discovered that there were no vacancies in the hotels. So we decided to take a shortcut through the farm country to the city of Eisenach. At the crossroads, we encountered a policeman who smiled and waved to us. After a while, we were in Eisenach, where we found a fine and reasonable hotel. We were tired and needed some rest. But before taking a rest, my wife and I went to the city to find the closest church and the time of the Sunday services. We found an ancient and beautiful church called Nicolaikirche, which was built by Roman Catholics a long time before the Reformation. Following the Reformation, it became an Evangelical (Lutheran) Church.

From the church, we went to the town's market, where we discovered a beautiful monument built by the citizens of Eisenach in memory of Martin Luther, the great reformer, who stayed in the city from 1498-1501 as a young student. The house, which then belonged to the Cotta family, is now called the Lutherhaus. The inscription on the monument reminded us of the fact that Luther spent ten months in the historic Castle of Wartburg following the Diet of Worms in 1521. The castle is elevated six hundred feet above the city of Eisenach. During his stay there, Luther translated the New Testament from the Greek language into German.

After exploring the market square of the city, we went to see some of the adjacent streets, looking for antique shops and galleries of art. Then, after having some good coffee and cake, we returned to our hotel.

The following day, Sunday, June 17, after having a late breakfast in the hotel's restaurant, all four of us went to the church (Nicolaikirche) for the ten o'clock service. After attending evangelical church services in Nuremberg two years before, I did not know what to expect.

When we entered the historic church about 9:45 a.m., most of the seats were already taken. A few minutes before the service began, only standing places were available. I could not believe my eyes. While attending Laurenzkinche (St. Laurence Church) in Nuremburg in the summer of 1988, I saw only about fifty persons attending the main service in the church, which could accommodate about four thousand persons. With the exception of our son Joseph, no one in the church was under the age of fifty. Here, in Eisenach, all ages of people were represented. There were infants in their mothers' or fathers' arms; children, teenagers, young men and women, middle-aged people, and older persons. Obviously, the church had no nursery, but no one was disturbed by the presence of the infants in the congregation.

As the church organist began to play the fine pipe organ, I was wondering if Johann Sebastian Bach and his parents, who were natives of Eisenach, have worshipped in this church and enjoyed the organ music. The organ music and singing were uplifting. During the sermon hymn, the children and younger teenagers went to Sunday school rooms for a short instruction. Shortly after the sermon, they returned to the church to take part in the Communion service.

The piety of the congregation, the prayers, the organ music, the hymns, and the sermon touched me very deeply and prepared me for the Holy Communion. When the Communion time came, my family and I went toward the altar. In accordance with the Lutheran liturgy, we formed a large circle before the altar to receive Holy Communion. The ministers stood in the middle of the circle and administered the Sacrament, a beautiful symbol of unity. The service lasted one hour and thirty minutes. No one left the church before the service ended, and no one seemed to complain about the length of the service.

After we left the church and walked to the hotel, I wondered why the Evangelical churches in Nuremberg are almost empty on Sundays and the church in Eisenach is packed with people. During lunch, we became aware that we were in East Germany, the Communist part of Germany. The uniformed man whom we saw in late afternoon yesterday as we drove toward Eisenach must have been a border guard, but seeing our West German car, he waved to us and did not stop us to check our documents.

It appeared to me that the wealth of West Germany made the people forget easily about their dependence on God and need for the church. That is why the churches are empty in Nuremberg (West Germany) and full in Eisenach.

In the afternoon, while our sons made an excursion to the Castle of Wartburg, my wife and I explored the old city and admired the architecture of the ancient and historic buildings. We also witnessed a mass confrontation between the military police (storm troopers) and some university students. The confrontation ended peacefully--the students ended their demonstration and left the market square.

We returned to the hotel toward evening. Soon, our sons came back from their long walk to the Castle of Wartburg. They enjoyed visiting the castle and were surprised that Martin Luther lived in a rather small room during the time he translated the New Testament.

On Monday, June 18, we exchanged some of our money for East German marks, did some shopping, and left the city of Eisenach heading toward Poland. As we drove east, we passed by the well-known cities of Mohra, Gotha, Erfurt, Weimar, Jena, and Karl-Marx Stadt. As we traveled across the country, we noticed that the farmland was taken care of quite well, but we did not see private farms. All land belonged to collective farms. There was so much farmland on each side of the highway, and the towns and villages were rather far away from each other. I began to reflect on the old German political tendency of *Drang nach Osten* (Push toward East), which Hitler rehashed and used as one of his aggressive slogans. There was so much space, both for farming and for building new villages and towns. Why did Hitler and his Nazi cohorts start World War II in the name of the *Lebensraum* (the living space)?

As I continued driving on the highway toward Dresden, it occurred to me that in the summer of 1939 the Nazi Panzer divisions and Wehrmacht divisions were rolling on the same highway toward the Silesian border of Poland.

At about 4:30 p.m., we reached the historic city of Dresden. It was time to look for a hotel. As we drove toward downtown, we noticed a small sign advertising bed-and-breakfast lodging in a suburban villa. We went to the villa and found good accommodations.

After having dinner at the villa, we started to explore the city, which lies on both sides of the Elbe River. As we walked through the northern suburbs of the city, we were struck by the beautiful orchards and flower gardens which surrounded beautifully built homes and impressive villas. Before we returned to our overnight accommodations, we crossed the bridge over the Elbe River and took a look at a small section of the downtown area.

The city of Dresden originated from a Slavic settlement. The German population began to settle in Dresden in the thirteenth century. The city became the official residence of the electors, and later, the kings of Saxony. It occurred to me that Augustus II "The Strong" and his son, Augustus III, who were electors of Saxony, became Polish kings. However, during their reign they showed more interest in Saxony than in Poland. Therefore their reign was greatly detrimental to the Kingdom of Poland. The Poles have never been proud of them.

As a clock collector, I became also aware that the most beautiful porcelain clocks came from Dresden. They are known as Dresden clocks. Tradition has it that Augustus II, who was always in need of money, ordered his subject, Johann Friedrich Bottger, an alchemist, to produce gold from inferior minerals. In his attempt to produce gold, Bottger produced porcelain out of white clay called *kaolin*.

The king was pleased with his alchemist's work and established a porcelain factory in the town of Meissen, which is located fourteen miles from Dresden. The factory flourished and produced a very fine porcelain that is very similar to that of China or Japan. Today, as in the past, Dresden clocks and other objects of art made of Dresden porcelain are very precious and are sought aggressively by art collectors.

On the way back to the villa in which we had our overnight accommodations, we came across a two-story house on a large lot which was grossly neglected. Its windows were broken and the yard was full of garbage. The surroundings and the condition of the house clashed with its lovely architecture. Needless to say, the house was vacant. It appeared to me that the last occupants of the house were Russian soldiers. In my youth, I had seen many houses in Poland in the same shape after the Russian troops had vacated them at the end of World War II.

My wife suggested that we should inquire into the possibility of buying the house and restoring it. So we looked around the neighborhood to see if somebody would give us some information. We noticed that across the street there was a man doing masonry work on his house. We walked to him and asked him whether the house which we liked was for sale. He explained to us that the house--like many other abandoned houses in Dresden--was in the hands of the city government, which would gladly sell the house on the condition that if the owner or one of his heirs would come from West Germany to claim the property it would go to the rightful owner. After hearing this explanation, we lost all interest in the house.

## Chapter II

The following day, Tuesday, June 19, we went to the downtown of Dresden. We were impressed by the historic buildings of this famous capital of the Kingdom of Saxony. The royal palace, which is being restored, is one of the most beautiful royal residences in Europe. Even though during World War II bombs and artillery fire damaged the city very seriously, we did not see any signs of war. Before we left the city of Dresden, we bought some food, fruit, and soft drinks for our snacks in the car.

At about 11:00 a.m., we said goodbye to the beautiful and ancient capital of Saxony and resumed our journey toward Poland. The highway east of Dresden was very poor and we had to take many detours through small towns and villages. This slowed our journey considerably but gave us a chance to see the countryside and to visit old churches and other points of interest along the way. As we passed through the town of Oppach, we came very close to Czechoslovakia and saw the billboards inviting travelers to that country. Soon, we were approaching the city of Görlitz, which is on the border between East Germany and Poland. But before we reached Görlitz, we stopped in a small town to buy a large quantity of canned meat and fish because we did not know if these things would be available in Poland. The prices of food were very reasonable in East Germany and food was plentiful in the stores, even though at times we saw people waiting in line to buy food.

In Görlitz, we crossed the border between East Germany and Poland. The city is divided by the Nysa River into two sections -- German and Polish.

The Polish part of the city is called Zgorzelec. When the German officer of the border guards checked our passports and visas, I was relaxed, but when the Polish officer was given our documents, I felt very nervous. I did not know what to expect from the border guards of my native land which I left thirty-three years ago as a *persona non grata*. When the officer asked me something in Polish, I did not understand him at first. Only after he repeated the question and added the comment, "You understand Polish, don't you?" did I respond in Polish. Our documents were in perfect order and we were asked to proceed to the next officer, who asked us about the content of our luggage and the amount of United States money which we carried on us. He accepted our declaration without question and did not ask us to open the trunk of our car. We were grateful for his consideration and drove into the Polish part of the city. On the Polish side of the city, everything was brighter than in East Germany. The road was better, and the people, especially the women and children, were better dressed. Reacting to this change, my wife exclaimed, "Look how colorful and well-dressed they are!" For some reason, the streets of the city through which we drove were full of life and activity.

Before we left the city of Zgorzelec, we stopped at the first bank on our way to exchange some of our currency into Polish zlotys. For one hundred United States dollars, we received about one million zlotys. We became instant millionaires. After exchanging our currency, we took the shortest highway to Cracow, where my stepmother and brother Klemens expected us any day. Since the death of Klemens' wife five years ago, my stepmother had been keeping house for him. The highway was of an excellent quality and reminded me of West Germany highways. I was gratified to see that road signs and symbols were of the same kind as in West and East Germany. On each side of the highway grew linden trees planted by the highway department. They were very pleasant to the eyes. At the rest areas, small businessmen operated grills and field kitchens to feed hungry travelers. We also noticed stands with fruit and mushrooms. Capitalism is taking hold in Poland.

In the late afternoon, we were very close to the city of Legnica, which was to the left of the highway. To the right of the road I noticed a sign which pointed to the town of Legnickie Pole (Lenica's Field). All of a sudden, it occurred to me that in the thirteenth century Polish Prince Henry the Pious of Silesia fought a decisive battle against a Mongol invasion there. He stopped the invasion of the Mongols but lost his life at the battle at Legnickie Pole in 1241. His saintly mother ordered the construction of a church on the spot where the prince died. We visited that church and read the Latin inscriptions on its walls which describe the tragic events of the past. We were also given a tour of another church, a very large church, which was built by a group of Benedictine monks.

Since evening was coming, we decided to go to the city of Legnica and look for a hotel. Soon, we found a newly-remodeled tourist hotel. The receptionist told me that she had two prices for hotel rooms; one for Polish guests and another for foreign guests. The price for a room for foreign guests was twice as much as for Polish guests. Since I was born in Poland, she decided to give us a domestic rate. I appreciated her kindness.

In the evening, we visited the old city and its magnificent castle which withstood the assault of the Mongols after the death of Henry the Pious.

## Chapter III

Early in the morning on Wednesday, June 20, we left the city of Legnica and headed toward Cracow. The weather was beautiful and the highway was not too busy. We drove through Wroclaw, Opole, and Katowice. By noon, we were nearing Cracow. We reached the suburbs of Cracow at about 1:00 p.m. As we drove through the suburbs, we were looking for a gas station because our gas tank was getting low. We passed a gas station without noticing it. Gas stations tend to look different in every country. We were not used to the way Polish gas stations looked and that is why we did not notice it. When we went to the gas station, we learned that unleaded gas is scarce in Poland. It can be found only in larger cities. I began to worry. At the same time, I noticed that other drivers whose cars used unleaded gas carried extra containers in their trunks and filled them every time they had a change. I went to the gas station office and inquired about the possibility of buying an extra container. An attendant told me that he had sold the last one the day before. I saw German motor oil at the station and I bought one gallon of it because that was the smallest unit available at the station.

Since the Holiday Inn hotel was near the gas station, we stopped there for a moment to exchange some of our currency. For curiosity's sake, we asked about rates for a room with two beds. The answer was $150.00 per night. The rooms were beautiful but also very expensive.

The taxi drivers at the Holiday Inn parking lot gave me excellent directions to my brother's residence in the southern suburb of Cracow. Shortly after 3:00 p.m., we were in front of my brother's house. His youngest son, Johnny, noticed our German car and opened the gate to the driveway. As I drove in, my brother Klemens appeared in the yard with a loaf of bread and a dish of salt -- symbols of hospitality. I broke off a piece of bread, dipped it in the salt, and consumed it. We both had tears in our eyes when we hugged and kissed each other on both cheeks according to Polish custom. Soon my stepmother, Klemens' older son Christopher, and Christopher's wife came out of the house. We were hugging and kissing each other. I greeted my stepmother as I always did, by kissing her hand and cheeks and hugging her. She cried tears of joy. I introduced my wife and our sons to her and to Klemens and his family. It was a very joyful and emotional reunion after thirty-three years.

Soon we entered my brother's new and spacious house and were invited to the dining room for a late lunch. Knowing that Polish hospitality is unthinkable without food, I did not attempt to explain to my brother and stepmother that we had already had lunch at noon. As we sat around the dining room table, we talked about our lives and the most recent changes in Poland. Things changed so fast and so unexpectedly in Poland. No one anticipated anything like that would happen. The Communist government in Poland lost its credibility and power. A new and democratic government took over. Under the new government, there is a great degree of hope for rebuilding of the Polish economy and other aspects of national life.

During our conversation in the dining room, I learned that my brother Klemens, who for most of his life worked as a geologist and supervised drilling for minerals in various parts of the country, had changed his work and is now employed by the coal industry. His two sons work as electrical engineers in the local power plant. The youngest son is still in school. In order to protect his savings from inflation, Klemens invested in a second house, which was constructed in a hurry on his property. His oldest son will occupy it soon.

Our conversation around the table lasted until dinner time. In spite of her eighty-five years, my stepmother prepared for us an excellent dinner, which for us was our fourth meal. We consumed it with gratitude. During the dinner and following, we talked about other members of the family--living and deceased--and recollected many episodes of our lives in the past. I spoke more than anybody else because I had to serve as an interpreter for my Polish-and-English-speaking family. The time went very fast.

It must have been midnight when we decided to retire for the night. Fortunately, my brother had taken one week off from work, so he did not have to get up early the next day. We slept very well on comfortable beds with very large pillows.

Thursday morning, June 21, following a very enjoyable continental breakfast, we decided to visit the oldest part of the city of Cracow. Since I had learned from my brother that no motor vehicles are allowed in the historic seciton of the city, I asked my brother's youngest son, Johnny, to accompany us and show us where to find parking for our car. He was eager to go with us.

With Johnny's help, we found a place to park our car within a short distance of the old part of the city. After parking the car, I went to the newspaper stand to buy a parking permit. Then all five of us walked up the hill to the royal castle called Wawel. From a short distance away, it appeared as beautiful as ever. I had visited it on numerous occasions during my graduate studies at Jagiellonian University. At that time, I was a very young man. After thirty-three years of being away, and after visiting many royal castles in various countries of Europe, Wawel was still as beautiful as ever, or even more beautiful.

Soon we were on the top of the hill and entered the castle's ancient courtyard. As we explored it, we were reminded by numerous inscriptions of the antiquity of the castle. The first stronghold on the castle hill was built by the legendary Polish prince Krak in 700 A.D. The main part of the castle was constructed in the twelfth century. Other parts of it were added by various monarchs. St. Stanislaw's Cathedral was soon built next to the castle and consecrated in 1359. In this cathedral, the kings of Poland were crowned, and when they died, they were buried in it.

We spent most of the day visiting the royal castle and the cathedral. We could not stop admiring the beauty of architecture, painting, sculpture, ancient furniture, and other national treasures. Before we left Wawal, we descended into the basement of the cathedral to visit the tombs of the kings and national heroes. Among these tombs were the tomb of John III Sobieski, who at the head of Austrian and Polish armies halted at Vienna the Turkish invasion of Western Europe in 1683, and the tomb of General Tadeusz Kosciuszko, who fought for the independence of the United States and became one of the Revolutionary War heroes.

From the royal castle, we walked toward the center of the city. Our way took us into the neighborhood of Jagiellonian University, which was established by Casimir the Great in 1364 and is the second oldest university in central Europe. I felt proud

Chapter III

to be a graduate of this great university.

As soon as we reached the market square, St. Mary's Church (*Kosciol Mariacki*) appeared in front of us. While looking at the beautiful thirteenth century church, my wife and our sons were struck by the unevenness of its towers. They wondered why one tower was taller than the other. I explained to them that according to an old legend, two master masons--who happened to be brothers--competed with each other in building the towers. One of the brothers, who must have been a better mason, overtook his brother and raised his tower faster. The brother who fell behind in construction became so jealous that he secretly committed the crime of fratricide by pushing his brother from the tower and blaming the fall on his brother's carelessness. The killer completed his tower to the very top and his brother's tower was left unfinished. The carpenters constructed a roof over it and in such an unfinished state it remained.

After viewing it from a distance, we came close to St. Mary's Church and waited to hear, from the tower of the church, the trumpeter's trumpet call, which he plays every hour. Soon he began to play, and then, as usual, he abruptly interrupted his music. He did this for a historical reason. When the Mongolians invaded Cracow in 1241, the trumpeter who then played the trumpet call was killed by a Mongolian arrow before he com-

St. Mary's

pleted his trumpet call. In memory of that heroic trumpeter, all the trumpeters from that time on are accustomed to interrupt their call abruptly.

After hearing the trumpeter, we entered St. Mary's

Church to pray for a moment and to visit it. Since our son Joseph and I spent a part of our summer vacation in 1988 in Nuremberg, Germany, where we learned to admire some masterpieces of art by Veit Stoss (Wit Stwosz), I led my family to the main altar, the principal work of the artist. The sculpture of the altar, in its center, represents the Dormition of the Blessed Virgin Mary in the presence of the Apostles. On the peripheries of the altar and above the central scene there are other religious carvings. The great sculptor completed his work in 1489. This beautiful altar remained at St. Mary's Church for five centuries until the Nazis removed it and took it to Germany in 1939. After the defeat of Nazi Germany in 1945, the altar was discovered in a tunnel under the city of Nuremberg and returned to its former place.

From St. Mary's Church, we walked to the fourteenth century Drapers' Hall *(Sukiennice),* located in the center of the market square and used for small businesses and the city museum. It was cool and windy, so we decided to have some coffee and cake in the Drapers' Hall. My wife and I (our sons were more interested in visiting small shops in the Drapers' Hall than in having cake and coffee) sat at an outside table and had an excellent cake (torte) and coffee. While we enjoyed our treat, we watched passersby and the flocks of pigeons which were fed near us.

Having finished our coffee, we went to the Drapers' Hall to see the stores. We were overwhelmed by the variety of merchandise. Most of the stores featured ladies' clothing, not only the European style of clothing but also the country's regional costumes, which tend to be bright and very colorful. In many instances, the stores sold products of cottage industry, such as woolen blankets, sweaters, toys, and gifts. Our sons bought a hand-carved game of chess for about four dollars. We could not believe how inexpensive it was.

Toward evening, we went to visit my first cousin and her daughter, who live in Cracow. As we entered their apartment, we discovered that it was full of visitors. A number of relatives were also visiting them. There was a small family reunion. After thirty-three years, it was necessary to get reacquainted with one another. All of us had changed to a great extent psychologically as the result of new experiences over the years. Also, we had to get used to the changes in our external appearances. After a certain age, most of us had experienced an expansion of our bodies and our hair had started to get gray.

One of my cousins, a university student whom we met there, was in the process of obtaining her student visa to the United States. She will stay with her grandmother in Florida and attend one of the universities in that state. She was very eager to learn from us as much as possible about our country.

In the evening, we returned to our quarters in my brother's home, where my stepmother waited for us with a big Polish dinner. The rest of the evening we spent again in the family circle, enjoying each other's presence and mutual conversations. We also made plans to visit the former Nazi concentration camp in Auschwitz *(Oswiencim)*, which is not far away from Cracow.

## Chapter IV

The following day, which was Friday, June 22, we had an early breakfast and then started on the way to Auschwitz. I had never visited that infamous concentration camp before and knew about it only from the narratives of some former inmates who survived it, from a number of books which I had read in the past, and from documentaries which I watched in the United States. As the result of this information, I had formed a mental picture of the concentration camp. On the way to Auschwitz, I was wondering whether my mental image of the camp and its reality would come close together or not.

Soon, we entered the city of Oswiencim (Auschwitz) and asked for directions to the former concentration camp. According to the directions, we proceeded to the outskirts of the city, where road signs led us to the camp. We had our first view of the concentration camp from the road. What we saw was a series of brick buildings which resembled a military base. There was nothing sinister about the buildings with the exception of the high barbed wire fence which surrounded them and carried a high-potency electrical current, and the watch towers located on the periphery of the camp.

Before we entered the grounds of the concentration camp, I noticed a nun walking on the side of the road. It occurred to me that she might be one of the sisters who lives in the controversial convent near the camp. I pulled to the side of the road and introduced myself to the sister. I told her that Father Joseph Wdowiak from Clarksburg, West Virginia, who died last spring, had painted on canvas Stations of the Cross as his personal gift for the chapel in the convent. Shortly after completing the stations, he wrote to the superior of the convent to arrange the shipment of the paintings, but he did not hear from her. He was under the impression that nuns who were forced to abandon the convent and move to another place no longer needed the Stations of the Cross. I gave the nun my calling card and suggested that if the superior needed the paintings for the chapel she might write to me so I could contact Father Wdowiak's sister.

In a moment, we were in the large parking lot built after the war to accommodate tourists. It was already noontime, so we went to the tourist center for lunch. Following lunch, we bought tickets to visit the former concentration camp, which the Polish government has converted into a museum.

We entered the grounds of the concentration camp through the main entrance, which was once barred by a large iron gate. The gate is still there. Over the gate, the motto of the Auschwitz death camp is written in steel: *Arbeit macht frei* (Work sets free). Once we were on the grounds of the camp, we visited many of the large buildings in which the prisoners were kept. In the basements of the buildings there were cells for solitary confinement. Most of these cells had no windows. In one of these cells, a number of candles were burning. It was the cell in which Father Maximilian Kolbe, a Franciscan priest, died for a fellow prisoner.

As a founder of the Franciscan Centers of the Immaculate Mary in Poland and Japan, which promoted Christianity through publication of books, periodicals, and newspapers, Father Kolbe was arrested by the Nazis in the early part of World War II and eventually placed in Auschwitz. When one of the prisoners escaped and the Nazis were selecting every tenth prisoner to be killed, Father Kolbe decided to take the place of a fellow prisoner who stood next to him in line. While other prisoners chosen to die were shot at the execution place, Father Kolbe was placed in solitary confinement without food and water. Ten days later, he was still alive. The Nazi physician then injected poison into the priest's body, which terminated his life. The man whose place Father Kolbe took survived the horrors of Auschwitz and returned to his wife and children. A number of years ago, he appeared at the canonization ceremonies at the Vatican during which the martyr of Christian love, Father Kolbe, was proclaimed a saint of the church.

One of the large buildings on the camp grounds served as a storehouse for women's hair, which the administration of the camp sold to the war industry. When the Russian Army liberated Auschwitz, seven tons of hair were still in the storehouse. The same amount of hair remains there today for visitors to see.

## Chapter IV

As we walked from building to building, we came across the "Wall of Death" where prisoners were executed by the SS firing squad. Nearby, we saw the long gallows constructed of rails.

The most fearful experience which we had was in the gas chambers. We walked into the chambers from a hallway, and a very thick door made of concrete closed behind us. At first, we were struck by the black walls of the chambers and a very oppressive atmosphere, but we went on to examine various rooms and to read the inscriptions on the walls. Soon, our sons went ahead of us and my wife and I walked together, but after a while we, too, went to separate rooms. All of a sudden, I had a weird feeling of being lost in these gas chambers from which there was no way out. I began to realize that the black walls of the chambers had heard the shouts of desperation of millions of people who were gassed there. If only these walls could talk, they would tell us things which human beings are not strong enough to hear.

After we left the gas chambers, my wife and I spoke about the feelings which we had in the gas chambers. As we compared notes, we discovered that our feelings and thoughts were very similar. What an interesting phenomenon!

From the gas chambers, we walked a short distance to see the crematoria where the bodies of millions of prisoners were cremated and the ashes dumped into the rivers and lakes. The ovens and the chimneys of the crematoria were built for a mass extermination of human beings.

As we walked out of the crematoria, we were all silent. Each of us was attempting to realize what happened there. We were attempting to comprehend the immensity of the crimes against humanity. We were asking ourselves the question, "Why all this?"

We saw a small gallows in front of the crematoria and went toward it. The inscription at the gallows stated that Rudolf Höss, commandant of the concentration camp, was hanged there as a person who was responsible for the death of millions.

Can any man be made responsible for such a deed? No, of course not. Höss was only one of the commandants of Auschwitz. He and others followed the orders of Heinrich Himmler, who in turn took orders from Hitler. Was Hitler, with his Nazi followers, responsible for the horrors of Auschwitz? While I reflected, it appeared to me that even Hitler, his followers, and the German nation could not be made totally responsible for Auschwitz and other concentration camps. The crime is too great to be attributed to a relatively small number of people. The responsibility goes far beyond Hitler, far beyond his followers, and far beyond Nazi Germany. After all, the Nazi ideology is not an exclusive product of Hitler, nor of Germany. It was born, grew, and developed in the midst of European Judeo-Christian culture and civilization. Most of the important elements of this ideology have very deep roots in the culture and civilization of all the countries of Europe and Asia Minor.

The principles of this ideology had been known and practiced quietly and sporadically centuries and even millennia ago until they crystalized as a philosophy and movement and, as such, erupted with a demonic power in our century. It happened to erupt in Germany, but it might have erupted in any country of the western culture and civilization. Thus, Rudolf Höss, Heinrich Himmler, Adolf Hitler and his Nazis were responsible for the crimes against humanity but they were not totally responsible. To a great extent, they were agents and instruments of the sinister power whose growth and development were tolerated for centuries and millennia in the Judeo-Christian culture and civilization. Therefore, all the nations of the western world share in the responsibility for the crimes against humanity committed during World War II. These were my thoughts as we stood in front of the crematoria and near the gallows on which Rudolf Hoss died for his part in the crimes against humanity.

Before we left the place of execution of Rudolf Höss, I mentioned to my family that a long time ago I read his extensive autobiography and it moved me to tears.* In this biography, Höss confesses that he was born into a very fine Christian family and attended church regularly. He lost his faith as a teenager through the bad example of his priest. During his adult life, he was an atheist. During his imprisonment in Cracow, Poland, he met a zealous priest who attempted to minister to

*Autobiografia Rudolfa Hossa Komendanta Obozu Oswiecimskiego,* Wydawnictwo Prawnicze, Warszawa 1990. See the original: *Kommandant in Auschwitz. Autobiographische Aufzeichnungen des Rudolf Hoss.* Stuttgart 1958.

him. Soon they became good friends. Through the grace of God, the prisoner regained his faith, repented, confessed his sins, and received Holy Communion. He died reconciled with God and the church. Before he died, Höss wrote two very loving letters: one to his wife and another to his children. In these letters, he admits that the greatest mistake of his life was the fact that he uncritically accepted and carried out the orders of his superiors. He warned his children, in particular, not to follow his footsteps in this regard.

From the gallows where Rudolf Höss died, we walked toward the gate of the camp. On the way, I turned back a couple of times to take a better look at various parts of the camp. It occurred to me that the mental image of the camp which I had formed before seeing it differed from its reality. Physically, it was smaller than I had envisioned it. Morally, its evil transcended my imagination. At the same time, I became aware that until our visit to Auschwitz, I was convinced that Hitler and his assistants and followers were solely responsible for death camps and other crimes against humanity. Following the visit, I, as an heir of Western Judeo-Christian culture and civilization, became aware that all of us in the west are partially responsible for such evils.

Before we left the parking lot of Auschwitz Concentration Camp, we decided to take a look at Birkenau Concentration Camp, which is very close to Auschwitz. We drove to the gate of the camp and were amazed at its size. It was perhaps ten times larger than Auschwitz. The majority of the buildings were constructed of wood, which had begun to deteriorate. Crews of carpenters were engaged in the restoration of many buildings. We did not enter the grounds of Birkenau, but drove along the electric fence line and observed. We were told that as soon as the restoration of the camp was completed, it would be opened to visitors as another war museum.

From Birkenau, we returned to Cracow. Before going to my brother's home, we paid a short visit to Mrs. Janina Kremer, mother of Marta Kremer, a well-known artist from Buckhannon, West Virginia, and delivered a letter from Marta to her. Mrs. Kremer lives in the historic part of Cracow. Since the death of her husband, a very successful lawyer, she lives in a very large apartment full of the most beautiful antiques, paintings, and books. One of the prominent oil paintings is a very large picture of Marta's grandfather in the academic gown of the president of Jagiellonian University.

Not knowing that we were staying with my brother, Mrs. Kremer invited us to stay with her. We expressed our gratitude for her genuine hospitality and explained to her that we were staying with my brother.

After leaving the hospitable home of Mrs. Kremer, we returned to my brother's residence for a tasty dinner and a great evening with the family.

# Chapter V

Early in the morning on Saturday, June 23, we packed our suitcases, had a good breakfast, said goodbye to the dear ones, left my brother's residence, and drove east to visit our family home.

As soon as we left Cracow, we drove by the city of Nowa Huta, a city named after its main industry: foundries and steelworks. Nowa Huta was built with the help of the Soviet Union following the Communist takeover at the end of World War II. It was supposed to be a one hundred percent secular and Communist city in which there was no place for a church or religion of any kind. It was to be a city of workers, a perfect city, a city of the future. It was built in proximity to Cracow, the former capital of Poland, whose citizens are deeply rooted in Christian culture and Christian values and, as such, are politically conservative and anti-Communist. By building this new city, the Communist builders intended to restrict and, if possible, eliminate the influence of the highly cultural and intellectual city of Cracow on the Polish nation.

The Communist scheme backfired in two basic ways. First of all, the workers of Nowa Huta forced their will on the Communist regime by building a large church in the center of the city. Secondly, the Communist "perfect city", which was to be an example for other cities, polluted the air in the city and its environs. The chimneys of the foundries, steelworks, power plants, and factories began to spew dense smoke into the air, making it harmful to people, animals, birds, and vegetation.

It appears to me that the city of Nowa Huta has the most polluted air in central Europe. When we were driving through it, I experienced a terrible burning in my right eye. After a short while, I lost sight in it on account of excessive tears. I put my handkerchief to my eye and kept driving, using only my left eye. My wife experienced a dryness of her nasal passages and a headache. Our sons, who sat in the back seat of the car, were visibly unaffected. What an example of a model Communist city! Soon, we drove out of Nowa Huta into its suburbs and then into the countryside. The air was clean again and after a while my right eye returned to normal.

Our journey east was very pleasant. We drove through towns and villages and farmland. What was striking to me was the fact that Poland was changing her face. The old frame houses in the towns and villages were almost gone--replaced by rather large and modern brick houses. The old-fashioned barns covered with straw were also disappearing and impressive new ones taking their place. Wherever we went, new houses, barns, and other buildings were under construction. There was an air of urgency in the people's work. For me, it was very exciting to see my old country being rebuilt so well and so beautifully.

As we drove further and further east, we did not see anywhere neglected houses or shacks of any kind. All properties were well-kept. What I forgot, after thirty-three years in the United States, was that the Polish people love flower gardens in front of their houses, fences around them, and gates at the entrances to yards. Now, as we drove and observed houses to the right and to the left of the road, I was strongly reminded of all these things. For my wife and our sons, who were born and grew up in the United States, the size of the flower gardens and the variety of flowers were something new.

When I left Poland in 1957, most of the fences around the yards and the gates were made of wood. Now they are made of steel and are nicely painted. The gates are very elaborate, decorative, and artistic. It appeared to me that there is a competition in each town as to who will have the most beautiful flower garden, fence, and gate. I was impressed and very proud of my heritage.

Speaking of flowers, I am convinced that, for one reason or another, the Polish people, especially the Polish women, love, cultivate, and appreciate flowers more than most of the people in any country in which I have been. Even during the unusual hardship under the Nazi occupation of Poland and the early state of Communism, when there were shortages of the most basic goods, the people would deny themselves some important necessities and buy flowers.

Most of the fine highway on which we drove east was beautified with English walnut trees. The trees grew on each side of the parkway and their deep green color was soothing to a driver's eyes.

As we drove in our German car through the towns and villages, teenagers and children waved to us. They must have taken us for Germans. This was clear indication that the World War II hostility toward the Germans has disappeared in Poland. The Poles tend to forgive easily, even though they are good at remembering past history. I believe that the experiences of the Soviet Communism in Poland indirectly helped the Poles to reconcile, to some extent, with the Germans. Wherever we parked our car in one of the towns or villages and went to see something of interest to us, upon returning to the car we always found it surrounded by children and teenagers who admired it. Polish cars, like East German cars, are rather small and of very poor quality, hence the curiosity about and admiration of our German car.

In the early afternoon, we reached the town of Polaniec, in which many of my relatives live. The inhabitants of the town refer to it as a city because of its antiquity and on account of ancient royal laws and privileges which officially called it the city of Polaniec and its inhabitants citizens of Polaniec.

When we entered the suburbs of Polaniec, I looked at my watch and was amazed that it did not take us long to drive from Cracow to Polaniec. After living in the United States, the distances between various places in Germany and Poland were very short for me. In the United States, we are used to great distances between cities and cities, towns and towns, because we are a relatively young nation and we have so much vacant land. The old Europe has a very dense population and the distances between various locations tend to be shorter.

Since I have many relatives in Polaniec and its vicinity, I had a problem deciding in whose home we should stay during our visit. We had a number of invitations. After a short discussion with my wife, we decided to stay in the suburban hotel.

The hotel was modern and had a large parking lot. The receptionist in the hotel asked for our passports and offered us a family suite, which consisted of two large bedrooms, a kitchen, and a bathroom, at a fabulously low rate: six dollars per night. When she told me the price, I could not believe my ears. We took the suite and unpacked our suitcases. The rooms were clean and had very large windows.

Soon my wife was using the kitchen to prepare a hot lunch. Immediately after the late lunch, we drove downtown to visit some of my relatives. The first stop we made was at the home of my first cousin, Maryanna. When I left Poland, Maryanna was still a young lady. Now she is married and has grownup children and small grandchildren. After a while, her husband and their son returned home and we had an exciting conversation around the dining room table. Maryanna and her husband described to us the events which took place in the family after I left Poland. They spoke about those who had passed away, those who were born, and those who married. Maryanna and her husband live in the same house in which her parents lived. It is a large log house. During my youth, it was one of the largest houses on the street. Now, since most of the neighbors have built new houses, Maryanna's house is the smallest.

After visiting for about two hours, we left my first cousin's home and went to see two daughters of my father's first cousin. The older of the sisters is a widow, and the younger, who never married, is a retired school teacher. They live together very comfortably. The retired school teacher shared with us some details about our family's history. She has taken a special interest in our family's genealogy.

Since evening was coming, we decided to return to the hotel and go to bed early. As soon as we entered the lobby of our hotel, a middle-aged couple approached us and introduced themselves as our relatives on my paternal grandmother's side. They invited us to visit them in home, which was near the hotel. We accepted the invitation and went to their home for a while. We talked about the branch of the family they represented and enjoyed snacks and tea. It was a very pleasant visit.

## Chapter VI

On Sunday, June 24, our day began early in the morning with Holy Eucharist. After the service, we had a light breakfast and went to the cemetery to pray at the graves of our relatives. As we went from grave to grave, we came across a new grave in which my cousin, a priest, was buried. I had not been aware of his death. He was a professor of classical languages and had taught me Latin in the seminary for a number of years. He also preached at my first Solemn Holy Eucharist shortly after my ordination. Before we prayed for the repose of his soul, I explained to my family who the priest was and told them that he was a great man and priest, an enthusiastic teacher, and an excellent speaker. His name was Father Julian Jarzyna.

After visiting the old cemetery, we walked the streets of the downtown area to see the changes that had occurred in over thirty years in this old town, which traces its history to pre-Christian times.

First of all, I noticed that the market square had changed considerably. In the middle of the market square there is a traffic ring, with beautiful flowers in the center of the ring. The majority of the buildings in the market square are still pre-World War II. During my youth, there were stores in some of the buildings. Now these stores have been converted into dwellings. The Communist government forced the store owners to close their businesses by opening government-subsidized stores in the new section, the workers' section of town.

As I viewed the buildings on the east side of the market square, I recognized one of the buildings. During World War II, there was a small restaurant in it. How could I forget it? Following an unsuccessful raid of our guerrilla unit on the Nazis near Polaniec, I met, in this restaurant, one of my Jarzyna cousins, who bought me dinner and arranged for my transportation to the quarters of our group. After a hellish experience of a night battle with the Nazis and swimming across the Vistula River and miraculously surviving in the face of dense Nazi bullets, it was so nice to experience human warmth, care, and a hot meal.

After leaving the market square, we drove to the new part of Polaniec, which did not exist in my younger years. The building of this part of the town was subsidized by the Communist government of Poland. Most of these buildings are apartment buildings, office buildings, municipal buildings, stores, restaurants, a movie house, and a large hotel. This new part of the town predetermined the direction which the future development of Polaniec will go.

Following lunch in one of the new restaurants, we drove northeast to the town of Osiek, which, like Polaniec, has historical and legal reasons to be called "City". In spite of the fact it is located on a rather important highway, Osiek has never developed. As we drove toward Osiek, I pointed out to my wife and our sons various villages in which I was stationed as a member of guerilla units during World War II. I also showed them the village of Struzki, which was torched by the Nazis and ninety-five percent of its inhabitants burned alive or killed by gunfire. They were all buried in a mass grave at the parish cemetery of Niekrasow, which was visible from the highway on which we drove.

As we approached the town of Osiek, I looked at the fields of rye and wheat on the right and left sides of the highway and began to think about the past. Many memories came to mind. The fields of rye and wheat reminded me of a battle which our guerrilla group fought against the Nazi unit which controlled Osiek, and which we believed had captured our commanding officer and one of our men. Through wheat fields and rye fields like the ones before us, we charged at the Nazi positions amidst gunfire. I happened to be, at that time, in the field on the right side of the highway. A few yards to my left, a young member of our group, "Szkot", was mortally wounded. I saw his face full of pain as the medics carried him away. Soon we took the southern suburbs of Osiek, and fighting from house to house we pushed the Nazis out of the marketplace. They took defensive position behind the stone walls of the parish church on the periphery of town. As we were about to take the churchyard from the Nazis, we received a report that a large enemy unit was approaching Osiek from the direction of Sandomierz and we were forced to withdraw. On the way back, we took with us the body of our comrad-at-arms, "Cap", and learned that our commanding officer who was supposed to be in the hands of the Nazis was slightly wounded but had managed to escape capture.

As I recollected the dramatic events of the past, we entered Osiek, which had changed so much in thirty-three years. The small houses which were rebuilt of materials left after the fire in September 1939 had been replaced by very impressive new houses constructed of brick. I could not recognize the street which I had known so well. The street by which we entered the town brought us to the market square, which in my mind was large and spacious. Now it was very, very small.

From the market square, we took Koscielna Street and drove toward the parish church. Unlike the town, the church had not changed at all. It had the same tower, the same roof, the same stone walls, and the same belfry.

We walked into the church to pray. After a short prayer, I explained to my family that my parents were married in this church and I was baptized in it. Before we left the church, we all walked to the main altar, where we knelt down and said a prayer. As soon as we left the church, we met the assistant pastor, who greeted us very warmly and invited us to visit him at the rectory.

From the church, we went to visit my stepmother's sister, Janina Bernacki, who lives near the church. She was home and was surprised to see us at her door. She is a widow and has no children. She was married shortly before World War II and lost her husband, her mother, and her brother in an accidental explosion of an artillery shell.

After warm greetings, we were asked to the dining room for tea and snacks. As we sat around the table, Janina told us about her life, which had been rather harsh. After the tragic death of her dear ones, she managed to build a small house out of half-burned lumber from her parents' house and barn which were destroyed by the fire in September 1939. Years later, she saved enough money to build the modern brick house which she now occupies. A large flower garden beautifies the house, and the vegetable garden provides her with an abundance of potatoes, cucumbers, cabbage, and tomatoes. Janina is involved in church work and takes part in various pilgrimages to holy places.

At the end of our visit, I asked Janina to go with us to the cemetery. I wanted to pray at the graves of my mother and brother, who died when I was three years old. (My father remarried and I always called my stepmother Mother.) I was not quite sure about the location of my mother's and little brother's graves. Janina knew the location because she tended the graves.

As we approached the cemetery, two statues of angels placed on the top of the gate greeted us. When we entered the cemetery, I noticed a new monument with the name of my godmother's daughter, who had died recently. We prayed at her grave. Then we went to my dear mother's grave and prayed there for a while. My infant brother was buried with her. She died in the process of delivering him.

After praying at our dear ones' graves, we walked to see the rest of the cemetery. I discovered that the cemetery had been considerably enlarged since I was there thirty-three years ago. Numerous graves of German soldiers who died in September 1939 and were buried in the military cemetery outside the parish cemetery were now in the very center of the enlarged cemetery. Both the graves of the German soldiers and the white crosses on them were kept very well. I asked Janina who kept the graves of the German soldiers so well. She replied that the Polish school children keep the graves and periodically place flowers on them. What a beautiful gesture on the part of the children of Osiek, the children of the town which was burned to the ground as the result of the German invasion in 1939. Blessed be the Christian spirit of forgiveness and love!

Having visited the cemetery, we took Janina home and then drove to the town of Gaj, near Osiek, where I was born and grew up until the age of ten. The town has changed so much that I drove through it without recognizing it. After we came to the next town along the highway, I knew that we had gone too far. We turned back and drove very slowly. Only then did I begin to recognize the forest which grew near the town. Almost one hundred percent of the old houses and other buildings which I remembered as a young man had been replaced by new ones. New roads which were nonexistent in my days had changed the geography of the area. I felt like a stranger in my native town.

In order to inquire about some of our family's friends, I parked the car on the side of the highway, walked to one of the new houses, and knocked on the door. A lady opened the door and asked me in. I looked at the people in the house and they curiously looked at me. I did not know them and they did not know me. We were perfect strangers. However, after I told them who I was, friendly smiles appeared on their faces. They recognized my name, and the lady of the house said she had heard about me from her parents. A very warm conversation followed. Before I left the friendly people, I obtained directions to my family's friends' home.

Another surprise visit. This time, I was recognized by the lady, who was my classmate in grade school. Her children did not know me. I introduced my family to her and she introduced her children to us. Her parents, who were the best friends of my parents, had died some time ago and her husband had passed away a few years ago. Her daughter, who had just received a master of arts degree in pharmacy, expressed a desire to emigrate to the United States. I explained to her that before she could get a job as a pharmacist in our country, she would have to learn the English language and complete courses in one of the American schools of pharmacy. My explanation visibly cooled off her desire to emigrate.

Our next stop was at a house which I remembered so well from my childhood. It was an old log home that was considered during my childhood to be a haunted house. The Kos family who lived there was afflicted by great tragedy. Mr. Kos died rather early in his life. His wife raised their son. When the son was about twenty years old, he became involved in some illegal activities, for which he was arrested, tried, and sentenced to long-term imprisonment. During the early years of his imprisonment, some criminal entered his mother's house at night and murdered her. After the tragic death of Mrs. Kos, the house was unoccupied for many years. No one wanted to live in it or even come close to it. Then a group of gypsies occupied the house only during the winters. Now an elderly lady, Toska--who in her youth worked for my parents--lives there all by herself. She helped my mother in her work and in taking care of me when I was a child. I have very pleasant memories of her and wanted to visit her. Unfortunately, she was not home. I was disappointed and decided to come again.

In the meantime, we drove to the farm where I was born and spent my early childhood. It was the farm which my mother inherited from her parents. It was a lovely farm with a stream flowing across the land and in the proximity of a large forest. When I completed the third grade, my father inherited a large part of his parents' farm. It was larger and better than my mother's farm, so we moved to the new farm and leased the old. Eventually, when the Communist government imposed very high taxes on private farms, my parents sold the old farm to a neighbor.

The neighbor built a new house on the very spot where our farmhouse was. He also built a new barn and other farm buildings. The only thing which remained from the days of my childhood was the well. Everything else was gone. I could not recognize the place. It was no longer the home of my childhood. It was a strange place to me. After a short conversation with the new owners of our farm, we drove to the village of Gieraszowice to visit my sister Danuta and her family. During our childhood and teenage years, Danuta and I had always been close. A few years ago, she and her husband visited her daughter and my family in the United States.

The village of Gieraszowice, like other villages and towns in Poland, had changed beyond recognition. As we entered the village, I had to ask somebody on the street about the location of my sister's home. In a moment, we were in front of her home, and her daughter, Beata, opened the gate so we could pull into the driveway. Soon, my sister, her husband Tadeusz, and their family appeared at the yard to greet us. It was a joyful reunion.

Once we entered their large new house, we were ushered into the dining room for the customary hospitality. I was impressed by the abundance of food. My sister and her husband operate a medium-sized farm on which they grow vegetables needed so much in the surrounding cities. When our newspapers write about a shortage of food in Poland, they basically write about the cities. The people in the villages of Poland who farm have plenty of food. Economically, they are better off now than when I lived in Poland. If the new government of Poland will eliminate collective farming, which the Communists introduced by force, and permit the farmers to farm the way they want to, they will produce enough food for the nation and for export.

After visiting my sister and her family, we decided to see my brother Robert, who inherited my parents' farm in the village of Jeziory. On the way to Jeziory, we stopped in the village of Sulisawice to visit the parish church and pray at the adjacent cemetery for the repose of the souls of our dear ones. First, we went to the church, where the evening Holy Eucharist was about to begin in fifteen minutes. We all knelt on the marble floor and looked in silence at the magnificent edifice, built of stone in English Gothic style in 1876, which can accommodate, at one time, about 1,500 worshippers. As we stood there, memories of many pleasant moments came to me; numerous and glorious celebrations of Christmas, Easter, Pentecost, and other feasts, my confirmation, the first Solemn Holy Eucharist which I celebrated on Pentecost Sunday in 1952, and the sermons which I preached each time I visited my home parish church and the prayers which I offered to God for myself and others. Being in the church and recollecting the spiritual and supernatural experiences of the past was in itself a marvelous homecoming.

From the church, which is referred to as the new church, we walked to the old church, built also of stone in the Romanesque style in the thirteenth century. This church has been beautifully restored and its interior repainted since my youth. From time to time, it is being used for public worship and can accommodate about five hundred persons.

During World War II, the basement of the old church was used for the printing of a secret anti-Nazi newspaper, which, as a teenager, I helped to distribute. The newspaper's name was "Odwet", which in Polish means "revenge".

The large sacristy of the old church serves now as a small museum of the "Odwet" underground newspaper and the "Odwet" guerilla unit. Among the "Odwet" memorabilia, the photographs of its members were displayed. My sons discovered my picture, in clerical suit, in the midst of others. It was a gratifying experience for my family and for me. Many persons whose pictures are displayed there are no longer alive. Some died while fighting the Nazi aggressor; others died of natural causes. When I looked at the pictures of those who already had gone to the Lord, I prayed for the repose of their immortal souls and thanked God for the gift of life which He continuously gives to the rest of us. I also expressed my gratitude to the Almighty for my dear family who made the homecoming trip with me and for the privilege of serving Him as a priest.

As we came out of the old church with the intention of walking to the nearby cemetery, we faced the belfry, which reminded me of many joyful moments during my boyhood of climbing up its steps with other boys and ringing the bells before Sunday services. Many a time as we rang the large bells very enthusiastically, they pulled us up into the air. Thinking about these experiences brought to mind another recollection, which I shared with my family.

In the middle of World War II, the Nazis were running out of brass for their war industry. In order to remedy this shortage, they decided to rob the churches of their bells. Father Jan Budzinski, a pastor of our church at that time, organized a team of strong men and asked them to dismount all the good bells and bury them in the churchyard. The only bells which were left hanging in the belfry were the ones that were cracked and useless. By doing so, the priest and the group of men took a great risk. They jeopardized their lives to save the bells which summoned them and their families to church each Sunday and holiday.

The bells remained buried until the end of the war. Then they were unearthed and remounted. Now the bells once more resound in the whole parish and call the people to church to worship the Almighty God. They survived the inhuman and Godless Nazism and their sweet toll now announces the demise of cruel and atheistic Communism.

From the belfry, we walked toward the cemetery, which is adjacent to the churchyard. When we came to the gate of the cemetery, I asked my family to stop for a moment while I explained that we were standing on a man's grave. In a major part of his life, this man was a horse thief. Toward the end of his life, he changed his behavior and repented for his thievery. Before he died, he asked the pastor of the parish and his family to be buried at the entrance to the cemetery. His final request was granted and he was buried there as an act of utmost humility and expiation.

As we walked into the graveyard and kept walking the main path toward the grave of my father, I looked to the right of the path to see the tomb of my uncle, Wladyslaw Mazgaj, and his family. I could not find it. The tomb was built sometime before I left Poland. Now I could not fine it. I felt frustrated.

Before we reached the grave of my father, we came across a small section of the graveyard where a number of my comrades-in-arms were buried. They sacrificed their young lives in the fight against the Nazi aggressor. We paused for a moment in front of their graves and read their names engraved on an impressive monument. This special section of the cemetery was created with the burial of the chief of the popular resistance group “Odwet” and two of his associates. The chief’s name was Wladyslaw Jasinski.

I explained to my family that the chief was a charismatic and heroic leader. As a young teacher, and later on as a lawyer, Jasinski was always interested in young people. He was constantly eager to help children and youth to grow both physically and intellectually. When World War II began in September 1939, he organized a group of young men and with their help launched the publication of the underground newspaper “Odwet”. As time went by and the need arose to fight the Nazis not only with the printed word but with the arms of war as well, Jasinski organized a very effective guerrilla unit which he named “Jedrus”. This unit terrorized the Nazis in the whole region. As a teenager, I had the privilege to be involved both in the work of the underground newspaper and in the activities of the guerrilla unit.

Wladyslaw Jasinski was killed by Gestapo men January 9, 1943. Two other men who were members of the “Jedrus” group died with him on the same day: Antoni Tos (“Antek”) and Marian Gorycki (“Polikier”). All of them were buried in the same grave.

Among many others who were buried in this reserved part of the cemetery, “Cap” was the closest to me. His real name was Marian (Mieczyslaw) Gaj. He was much older and stronger than I and treated me as if I were his younger brother. His presence always projected a sense of security and safety.

He knew how to extricate himself from the most dangerous situations. I remember the day when he joined our group after escaping from the hands of the Nazis.

The night before, “Cap” had transported in his farm wagon, across the Vistula River, some weapons and ammunition and a small group of guerrillas. He and his passengers crossed the river to the west bank on the ferry and then proceeded by wagon to one of the remote villages where the weapons and ammunition were stored and the guerrillas had found a safe place to hide. After giving his horses a short rest, “Cap” returned to the ferry with the intention of crossing the Vistula River to return home before sunrise. As he was about to urge the horses to pull the wagon onto the ferry, a group of Nazi police which was hidden in the bushes surrounded the wagon and commanded "Cap" to raise his hands. He was unarmed and therefore had no choice but to follow the command. The police searched him and the wagon and did not find anything incriminating. Then the interrogation started. The commanding officer of the Nazi police unit wanted to know what "Cap" was doing away from home so late at night. "Cap" explained that he had been forced by a group of guerrillas to transport them into this area and now he was returning home. The officer accepted this answer as plausible and asked "Cap" where he had taken the guerrillas. "Cap" gave the Nazi officer the name of a remote village which was far away from the one to which he had actually taken them. The officer was euphoric and decided to lead his subordinates to that village. Before leaving, he tied "Cap's" hands behind him with a belt and ordered him to lie down face-up on the floor of the farm wagon. The officer left one of his policemen to guard the prisoner. The policeman sat on the farm wagon's seat and kept his loaded rifle directed toward "Cap".

After lying on his back for a moment, "Cap" became aware that the belt with which his hands were tied could be untied if he moved his hands long enough. Every time he had a chance, "Cap" moved his hands to release them from the belt. After a while, his hands became free. In order to distract the policeman's attention, "Cap" asked him for a cigarette. The policeman refused. "Cap" did not give up and asked for another favor. Since his winter coat and shirt had been unbottoned during the search, he asked the guard to button them because the air was cold. This time, the policeman agreed to help the prisoner. He leaned the rifle against the middle of his arm and reached out toward "Cap's" buttons. "Cap" took advantage of this. He grabbed the policeman's arms and then overpowered him and took his rifle. The roles were reversed. Now the Nazi policeman begged for his life. "Cap" was generous. After giving him a couple of kicks and calling him some unquotable names, "Cap" disappeared into the wicker bushes which grew densely on the banks of the Vistula. Of course, he took the policeman's rifle and ammunition with him. A couple of days later, he joined our guerrilla unit. During his service in the unit, he was brave to the point of heroism. He lost one of his eyes in one of our skirmishes with the Nazis and learned to fight with one eye. Toward the end of the war, he was killed by the Nazis in the town of Osiek.

After praying for the heroic souls of Wladyslaw Jasinski, "Jedrus", Marian (Mieczyslaw) Gaj, "Cap", and all the others who are buried there, we walked to the central part of the cemetery where my father, two of his brothers, and their parents are buried. On three sides of the stone monument, their names and the dates of their births and deaths are engraved. My grandfather and two uncles died before my days, my grandmother died during my boyhood, and my father passed away after I left Poland and was in the United States. I was unable to attend my father's funeral. The "Iron Curtain" did not permit me.

A couple of years before my father died, he visited me for the second time in the United States. Each of his visits lasted nine months. During these visits, we spent a great deal of time together and had a chance to get to know one another as grownup and mature men. I taught at St. John's Seminary in Bloomingdale, Ohio, at that time, and had most of the afternoons free to spend with him. The seminary administration assigned to him an apartment on the campus so we could be close to each other. He learned to follow the seminary schedule and daily attended eucharistic services in the chapel and took meals in the faculty dining room.

During summer vacation, my father and I traveled extensively. Among the places of interest we visited was Lackawanna, New York, where three of my father's brothers and their families lived and where my father also lived as a young man. He left Lackawanna for Poland in 1913. Upon returning to the city in 1964, he could not recognize it. He told me that in his days most of the streets in the city were unpaved and boardwalks were on each side of the streets.

My father's reunion with his brothers was very warm and emotional. They recollected the events of their youth at home and the time when they had last seen each other. It was a joy to see them enjoy each other after so many years of separation.

As we stood at the grave of my father, I thought about his reunion with his brothers in Lackawanna, about how he taught me to read and pray, about his example of prayer when he visited me at St. John's Seminary, and about the last time we had seen each other at John Kennedy Airport in New York when he was boarding a jet to return to Poland. I also thought that no human being becomes grownup enough, mature enough, or old enough not to miss his or her parents.

At the end of our visit to the graves of our dear ones, we said a prayer for the repose of their souls and returned to our car to drive to the nearby village of Jeziory to see my brother Robert and his family.

It took us about ten minutes to reach the village of Jeziory. As we approached the village, my heartbeat accelerated. The last time I had visited Jeziory--where I spent most of my childhood and youth--was in early June of 1957. Later that month, I left for the United States of America. Today, I was back in my hometown with my wife and our two teenage sons.

Even though the layout of Jeziory remained the same, new and spacious houses had replaced the old ones. As we entered the village, we noticed a group of young men standing on the corner of the street and talking. As they noticed our German car, they interrupted their conversation and fixed their eyes on us. We drove without stopping toward the other end of the village where I grew up.

Soon we were in front of my brother's farmyard. One of his sons opened the gate for us. In a moment, my brother Robert and his wife came out to greet us. There were many hugs and kisses. Before we entered my brother's home, I looked around at the yard and the farm buildings. Everything had changed. The farm buildings which my father's parents had built were no more. They had been torn down and replaced with large modern structures. The two-story brick house is twice as large as our old log house. The barns, storerooms, and garages are spacious and well-constructed. Even the fruit trees in the orchard were new. I could not believe my eyes. The doctrine of one of the ancient Greek philosophers that everything is in a continuous state of change made alot of sense to me at that moment.

As soon as we entered my brother's dining room, my brother's second son returned home. He told us that he was in the group of young men that we had passed and he had a feeling that we were driving to his home.

After having some snacks, which my sister-in-law served very generously, my brother and his wife took us on a tour of the farm buildings and the orchard. I was very impressed by what I saw. What impressed me most was the abundance of farm machinery, very modern and well-kept tractors, trucks, and other implements. When we went into the granary, I was shocked at the amount of grain which my brother kept there before the harvest. Our newspapers in the States write so much about shortages of everything in Poland, and there I saw so much grain. Soon I learned that the new Polish government of Mazowiecki imports grain, meat, and vegetables from other countries while the Polish farmers do not know what to do with their farm products. What a narrow-minded policy! Sometimes, great intellectuals have very little common sense or practical reason. This, in part, explains why Mazowiecki was rejected by the majority of Polish voters when he ran for the office of president of Poland.

From my brother's granary, we went to see his orchard, which was rather extensive. The fruit trees were young and well-kept. They were loaded with fruit. While walking through the orchard, I had a chance to look at the pond behind the main barn. During my youth, we called it a lake. It was large and deep then and had plenty of good fish. Now it was very small and muddy. Something had happened to the water. When I asked my brother about it, he explained to me that two other ponds in the neighborhood which once were deep and wide had dried out also. He attributed the disappearance of the ponds to the change of climate.

Before we left the orchard, I asked my brother Robert how he markets his fruit since the government imports fruit from other countries. He replied that he and his two sons truck the fruit to the large cities and sell it to people who need it. In such a way, he avoids a middle man and obtains larger profits. Only then did I discover that the main source of my brother's wealth is the fact that he is enterprising, physically strong, and has three hard-working persons helping him--his wife and two unmarried sons.

After visiting my brother and his lovely family, I felt proud of them for managing the family farm so well. When I visited the village of Jeziory the last time, in the spring of 1957, our neighbor was the most successful farmer in the village. Now my brother has acquired that honor. As time passes, the fortunes of various families go up and down. This seems to be a part of life.

Our next stop in Jeziory was at the home of my first cousin, Jan Mazgaj. Jan, his wife, and one of their married sons were in. In his letters to me, Jan had asked me to visit him as soon as possible because of his heart condition. He did not expect to live long. Even though Jan is my senior, we were very close before I left Jeziory to pursue my education. Even after I left our village and studied in the city, I used to see Jan during vacation time. When I celebrated my first Solemn Holy Eucharist in the parish church, Jan organized the outdoor festivities for the occasion. Now we had a chance to see each other and embrace each other after thirty-three years of separation. What a beautiful experience!

Soon I hugged Jan's wife and the rest of the family. My wife and our sons followed me in the warm family reunion. The unavoidable Polish hospitality followed. At the dining room table, I looked at Jan, his son, and his grandchildren, and saw in them many family features and characteristics. I am sure that he gazed at me and my sons in the same fashion. It was a very pleasant visit.

At the end of our visit, Jan and his family walked us to our car. I noticed two large passenger buses parked on the side of the large farmyard. What were the passenger buses doing there? Soon I learned that Jan and his sons provide a charter bus service for the area, a very encouraging sign of capitalism at work after so many years of Communism.

Before we returned to our hotel in Polaniec, we stopped to see my cousin, Thaddeus Lukaszek. Thaddeus's mother and my father were first cousins. When we pulled into his driveway, he was picking raspberries. Needless to say, he was surprised to see us. Nevertheless, he was grateful for our visit.

During my boyhood, Thaddeus was the most brilliant and inventive man I knew at that time, although he had no formal education beyond grade school. He was an expert in agriculture and horticulture. During World War II, when the Nazis took control of grain mills and prohibited the farmers to use them, Thaddeus constructed a very sophisticated mill which the people of Jeziory used freely to satisfy their immediate needs. Thaddeus endangered his life by providing such a service to the community.

It was already dark when we returned to our hotel. Since we were running out of unleaded gas and could not buy it in any of the neighboring cities, we decided to return to Cracow the following day to fill our gas tank. In the meantime, we needed some rest at the end of a very busy day.

## Chapter VII

On Monday, June 25, we got up early and started on our way to Cracow. As we drove the already familiar highway, we stopped in larger towns and searched for metal containers. In one of the towns, we found one twenty-liter container. In another town, we found two containers of the same kind. We paid the same amount of money for the two as we had for the first one. They must have been on sale. The containers were of an excellent quality, made in Poznan, Poland. I wondered why I never saw such fine containers in our country. What has happened to the quality of some of the American products?

Once we reached Cracow, we drove directly to the only gas station in the city--and probably in the whole region--which sold unleaded gas. At the gas station, we filled up the gas tank in the car and the three other containers which we had just bought. Now we had, altogether, 130 liters of unleaded gasoline with which to visit our relatives and explore the countryside.

After getting the gas, we drove to the royal castle Wawel to explore the dragon cave which is in the castle hill. The cave is located above the water level of the Vistula River. The image of the dragon, cast in brass, is placed at the entrance to the cave. Every few seconds, flames come out of the mouth of the dragon.

According to prehistoric legend, there was a vicious dragon in the cave in the castle hill during the time of prehistoric Prince Krak. Every time the dragon was hungry, he would come out of the cave and kill some people and some cattle and devour them. He terrorized the whole area. The prince's subjects begged him to kill the dragon. Responding to the people's pleading, the prince announced that he would give his daughter in marriage to any young brave knight who killed the dragon. But all of them, one after the other, were killed and devoured by the monster. Finally, a young son of a farmer came to the prince and volunteered to kill the dragon. The prince and his advisors were skeptical about the young man's abilities; nevertheless, they allowed him to try to fight the vicious dragon. The young man was happy to have his chance to get rid of the killer beast. He returned to his father's farm and began his preparations to kill the dragon. First of all, he butchered two calves, removed their intestines, packed their bellies with sulfur and salt, and stitched the incisions. Then he placed the carcasses of the calves near the dragon's cave. Soon, the hungry dragon came out. He swallowed the calves and returned to the cave satisfied. After a while, he experienced a terrible thirst. He went to the Vistula and drank and drank until his belly burst. Thus died the vicious killer dragon that lived in the cave under the castle. The young and ingenious man married the daughter of the prince and lived happily at Wawel Castle.

After visiting the dragon cave, we began our journey back to Polaniec. As we drove through Nowa Huta, our eyes again began burning due to the highly-polluted air. On the way back, we visited a magnificent residence which in the past belonged to the Radziwill family. Now it is used as an orphanage. We returned to our hotel in Polaniec in time for dinner. We had had a long and eventful day.

## Chapter VIII

On Tuesday, June 26, following an early breakfast, we drove to Osiek. On the way, I saw a directional sign pointing toward the village of Mikolajow. It reminded me of one of my grade school classmates who lived there. His name was Mroz. If I am not mistaken, his family was the only Polish family which lived in the German village of Mikolajow. The Germans who lived in the village came from Germany following World War I. They bought a large amount of rather poor land and built a village. The Mroz family refused to sell its land to the German settlers and became a part of the village. Through hard work and mutual help, the German settlers made a good living on their farms. They preserved their language and customs. They had their own church and grade school.

When Hitler came to power in Germany, the settlers in Mikolajow became his ardent supporters. Their support of Hitler was not limited to words and good will. They became the Nazi fifth column. In 1938, the agents of the Polish police, with the help of Mr. Mroz, intercepted shortwave coded messages which were being broadcast to Germany from the tower of the church in Mikolajow. Soon after, the secret radio station was seized by the police and the leaders of the fifth column were arrested.

When the Nazis invaded Poland in 1939, the settlers of Mikolajow collaborated with the invaders by creating confusion among the people in the whole area. Later on, they pointed out to the Nazi police Polish political leaders and activists.

If I am not mistaken, in the second year of World War II, the Nazi authorities relocated the German settlers from Mikolajow to the village of Gerlachow, near Sandomierz, where the soil was rich and the farm buildings large and well-constructed. The Polish farmers from Gerlachow were moved, by force, to Mikolajow.

As we drove toward Osiek, I narrated the above events to my family. In Osiek, we looked for flowers to place on my mother's grave. The flower shop was closed, so we were directed to the residence of the florist. While the lady florist cut the flowers in her garden, I engaged her husband in a conversation. We talked about the conditions of life in Poland. He was concerned with the excessive air pollution which resulted from the sulfur industry that developed very rapidly in the area after I left the country in 1957. He was fearful of the projected development of the industry. When I complimented him on his impressive residence, he replied that his home and other new homes in the area will be worthless when air pollution turns the beautiful part of the country into uninhabitable desert.

As I listened to this perceptive and intelligent man, I thought about my grade school, high school, and college teachers who glorified industry and saw the salvation of Poland in her industrialization. I wished they were here to hear what this man had to say about the reality of industry.

After we bought the flowers, we drove to the cemetery and, in the midst of prayers, placed them on my mother's grave. From the cemetery, we went to the shop of a stonemason who builds monuments. I made arrangements with him for the restoration of my mother's monument at the cemetery. Having done this, we drove to the city of Tarnobrzeg to visit my brother Zbyszek. Since he was still at work, we drove to the downtown area, parked the car, and walked to Jan Tarnowski State High School, which I attended as soon as the German troops were forced to leave the area (the war was still going on west of Tarnobrzeg). The high school which educated many generations of young people was no longer there; it was moved to a suburban location. The venerable high school building is being used now for the offices of the provincial government. The security man who stood at the main door of the building allowed us to enter it and wander around for a while.

I took my family on a short tour of the building. The classrooms in which I studied were divided and converted into small offices. The hallways remained the same and appeared to me much smaller than in the past.

From the old high school building, we walked to the Dominican Church, which also serves as a parish church. I explained to my family that each Sunday during the school year, even though Communist government ruled Poland, all the high school students gathered together in their classrooms, where the instructors checked attendance, and then walked together, two by two, under the leadership of the principal and the faculty, to the church for the service.

My wife and our sons were impressed by the size and beauty of the baroque church, which was richly endowed and decorated by the Tarnowski family. The Dominican monks whose monastery is adjacent to the church ministered in the church for centuries. After visiting the church and praying in it, we went to a nearby restaurant for a fine lunch (soup and pierogi).

As soon as we finished our lunch, we walked to the castle which, until the Communist takeover in Poland, was the residence of the ancient Tarnowski family. When I enrolled in Jan Tarnowski State High School, the high school administration used the central part of the castle for boarding some of the students. I happened to be one of the students who lived and boarded there. Since I had many pleasant memories from those days, I wanted my family to visit the castle and see the rooms in which I lived.

A lady whom we met in the office was very friendly and promised to give us a tour of the castle, but as soon as a couple of men entered the office and one of them said he was from Canada, she became very apprehensive about the tour and said to them that she had no keys to the rooms.When they left, she asked us to wait for a while and then telephoned one of the administrators who had the keys. When the administrator arrived in the office, he recognized me and reminded me that I had officiated his marriage to his wife before I left the country. He called up his wife and asked her to talk to me. She invited us to their home.

It was a joy to have him as a guide. He showed us the whole castle, including a very valuable library and the chapel. At the end of the tour, he explained to us that he and other administrators of the castle are reluctant to show it to strangers because some claim to be heirs or relatives of the Tarnowskis and want to take some valuables with them. The library, in particular, contained many valuable paintings and books.

Since the Communist government lost its control in Poland, many of the wealthy families who were deprived of their possessions by the government are now attempting to regain them through the courts of law. As we were walking through the castle's courtyard to return to the downtown area of Tarnobrzeg, some ladies who were watching their children play asked us if we were, by any chance, relatives of the Tarnowskis who had come to claim the property.

Before we reached the downtown, we made a left turn in search of the residence where my father's first cousin, Alexander Mazgaj, used to live and work at Koscielna 24. I had a hard time finding the place and then I realized that a new skyscraper is being constructed on Alexander's property. Alexander and his wife died about ten years after I left Poland. They were a very unusual couple. I lived with them for some time during my high school days. They were very talented musicians. She was a pianist and he was an orchestra conductor. Both of them studied music at the Budapest Conservatory, where they met. Alexander's father-in-law had a furniture factory in Budapest which the young couple eventually inherited. When Communists took control of Hungary for a short while at the end of World War I, Alexander and his wife were afraid to live in the country, so they moved to Poland. When I met them for the first time in Tarnobrzeg, just before the end of World War II, a group of Russian officers occupied their residence and the furniture factory was used as a meeting place for Russian soldiers. Huge latrines were built in their beautiful orchard, and the fences were broken. Most of the very exquisite furniture was confiscated by some high-ranking Russian officers and shipped to Kiev in the Soviet Union. Alexander and his wife were crushed and furious. They had left Hungry on account of Communism but Communism had followed them to Poland. Both of them hated and cursed communism with passion.

They were very lonely and sorrowful because their only son, who was my age, had drowned recently while swimming with his girlfriend in the Vistula River. In such an emotional state, it was no wonder that they received me with open arms. During my stay with them, they treated me as if I were their son. I will never forget our evenings together as they played duets--she on the piano, he on the violin or, more often, flute. They both spoke a number of foreign languages.

With the Russian troops in the country, the demand for fine furniture was nonexistent. Alexander began to produce church organs. It was very meticulous, laborious, and challenging work; however, it was crowned with great success. Alexander produced and sold a number of fine organs. In such a way, he made a very good living.

After my graduation from high school, Alexander and his wife had a very serious talk with me and proposed to make me their heir if I, in return, would agree to take care of them in their old age. Since I had plans to go to college and graduate school, I declined their offer. Both of them were disappointed and hurt. Our relationship cooled. After my priestly ordination, we resumed our relationship, which once again became warm and cordial.

From Koscielna Street where Alexander and his wife lived, we walked to the marketplace. We were impressed by the abundance of goods which people were selling and buying. There were stands with clothing, shoes, hats, hardware, motorcycles, fruit, and produce. Some of the wares were brought from the Soviet Union by Russian merchants. Other things came from Eastern Germany and other neighboring countries.

During my high school days in Tarnobrzeg, the marketplace used to be the farmers' market. Now it has changed its character and is being called *gielda*, whcih means something like stock market. I was told that before World War II and in the early stages of the war, this place used to be a Jewish cemetery. The Nazis converted it to a marketplace and used the tombstones for paving.

Out of curiosity, we wandered in the marketplace for a while. Before we left, we bought some fruit and vegetables at a very reasonable price.

From the marketplace, we drove to the suburban area of Tarnobrzeg to see my brother Zbyszek. It must have been about 5:00 p.m. when we arrived at the apartment building in which he lives. I parked the car on a side street and asked my family to wait for me until I found my brother's apartment. I had no trouble finding his apartment, but no one was at home. I was disappointed and decided to return to the car. As I walked back to the car, I noticed a large group of grade school children standing around the car, trying to communicate with my wife and our sons. Obviously, the children were attracted to our German car and then discovered that the passengers in the car did not speak Polish. Soon I was involved in translating the questions and answers which were coming from both sides. The children were very polite and well-behaved. Before we left, my wife gave them some candies and chewing gum.

Soon we were on the way back to Polaniec. We returned to our hotel in time for dinner. In the evening, we made preparations for our trip to Sandomierz.

# Chapter IX

On Wednesday, June 27, early in the morning, we were on the way to the city of Sandomierz. We stopped in Osiek for a moment to see Toska, who used to work for my parents as a maid during my early childhood. She was visiting her daughter and was very happy to see us. I explained to her that we had attempted to visit her in Gaj a few days ago but she was not at home. She knew about our attempted visit from the neighbors. We talked about the old days. She told me about my mother's personality and the color of her hair. Our younger son inherited my mother's blond hair.

After we left Osiek, we drove toward Sandomierz and made another stop in Koprzywnica. I wanted my family to see an ancient and beautiful church which was built during 1207-1218. It was constructed in the Romanesque style and then changed to the Gothic style. The church was built of stone by a group of Cistercian monks who came to Poland from Citeaux, France, in 1185. The monks used the church exclusively for their prayers and liturgy. Only in very exceptional cases were laymen admitted to the church. There was another church which the monks built nearby for the use of lay people who preferred it instead of the parish church.

At the present time, the large Cistercian Church serves as a parish church. The small church near the monastery and the parish church are no longer in existence. The small church was destroyed by order of an eccentric abbot who claimed that the small church obscured the view of the countryside from the windows of his residence. The abbot's name was Ossolinski. Some members of the order disobeyed the abbot and refused to have anything to do with the destruction of the church. They also petitioned the church authorites in Rome to remove the eccentric superior. The abbot was removed from his office and sent to another monastery for penance.

We admired the interior of the church, which can easily

accommodate about two thousand persons. The walls and arches of the church are not painted. They are built of pristine light stone which gives an impression of Spartan simplicity and beauty at the same time.

During our short prayer in the church, I thought about the generations of monks who chanted prayers for centuries. The walls and arches of the church had visible marks of wars, many wars. The structure of the church suffered from the Tatars, Swedes, Frenchmen, Austrians, Russians, and Germans.

After we left the church and started to examine its external architecture, I discovered that the tower of the church has been rebuilt. When I left the country, the church had no tower. The tower was destroyed in an artillery duel between the Austrians and Russians during World War I. The base of the tower was covered with a temporary roof. Under the very capable leadership of Father Jan Wiacek, pastor of the church, the tower was reconstructed from old drawings.

To my knowledge, the tower which was destroyed by the Austrian and Russian artillery was not original. The old tower, which was probably not original either, was destroyed during the Napoleonic wars in the first part of the last century. Then a new tower was built which was unlike the old one. This tower was designed by an architect from Cracow, who, if I am not mistaken, was hired by the eccentric abbot Ossolinski. Shortly before I left Poland in 1957, I did some researach in the parish archives; to the best of my recollection, the genesis of the architectural design of the tower occurred under the most unusal circumstances.

The architect summoned by the abbot arrived from Cracow at the Cistercian Abbey in Koprzywnica. Since he was a very busy man, he wanted to see the abbot as soon as possible. The monks told him the abbot was preoccupied with something very important and could not see him. They gave the architect a comfortable room and asked him to wait until the next day. The architect agreed. The following day, he again attempted to meet with the abbot, but a brother who guarded the entrance of the abbot's residence told him that his superior was busy and could not receive any visitors. The architect was disappointed and returned to his room. The next day, he went again to the abbot's residence. The brother told him the same thing as the day before -- the abbot was busy. At that point, the architect lost his temper and forcefully entered the abbot's rooms. He found the abbot in his library, sitting at the table and drinking wine. There was a pitcher of wine on the table and a glass of wine in the abbot's hand. The glass that the abbot held in his hand had no base. It was made in such a way that the person who was given it had to drink its contents to the last drop and then put it on the table cup down. In the old Polish, this kind of a drinking glass was called *kuslawiec*, which means "crippled one".

The abbot was not too unhappy to see the angry intruder and invited the architect to have a drink with him. The architect said he had wasted a lot of precious time waiting to meet with the abbot and now he would rather discuss business than drink. He asked the inebriated abbot about the shape of the tower which he wanted him to design. The abbot became very pensive for a moment, then drank the wine from the "crippled" wine glass, put it on the table upside-down, pointed to it, and said, "This is the shape of the tower I want you to design." The architect made a sketch of the glass, returned to Cracow, and designed the tower. Soon the tower was constructed according to this design. The present tower is a replica of that tower.

After telling my family the above story about the church tower, I had to tell another episode which I also discovered in the church archives. This episode demonstrated the narrow-mindedness and selfishness of the former citizens of Koprzywnica, which--perhaps because of these insufficiencies and limitations--never developed, but remained a small and insignificant town for centuries.

This is what happened a long time ago. The city of Osiek and the city of Koprzywnica competed for prominence with each other. A man committed a crime in Osiek. It was a capital offense. The court imposed a death penalty on him. The execution was to be carried out in Osiek. The city had no gallows. Therefore, the fathers of the city of Osiek sent a delegation to the fathers of the city of Koprzywnica and asked them if they could borrow their gallows for the execution of the criminal. The fathers of the city of Koprzywnica refused the petition and in a letter to the fathers of the city of Osiek stated, "We will not let you use our gallows because we have the gallows for ourselves and our children."

After we left the churchyard, I led my family to the wall which separates the monastery garden from the main street. At that wall, the Nazis executed many people. The marks of the bullets are still on the wall.

From the wall of the executions, we returned to our car and resumed our trip to Sandomierz. Before we left Koprzywnica, we had to cross a small river. As we entered a bridge, I remembered the day in 1943 on which the Nazi police (S.D.) almost ended my life and the life of my comrade-at-arms.

We were sent on some mission to Koprzywnica. In order to be less conspicuous, we left our bicycles with a friendly family in the western suburb and walked toward the churchyard, from which we could observe the quarters of the Nazi police. It was in the summer and on the day of Farmers Market in Koprzywnica. People were everywhere. My friends and I felt secure among the people. After we performed our mission, which might have been an observation of the police quarters, we walked toward the river, crossed the bridge, descended to the bank of the river on the right side of the bridge, took our shoes off, and soaked our feet in the water. We obviously had some premonition of danger because we did not soak our feet too long. Soon we were back up on the bridge and walking toward the church. Before we came off the bridge, we noticed a unit of Nazi police (S.D.) wearing helmets, carrying rifles, and running in military fashion toward the bridge. Fortunately for us, there were many people on the bridge walking in the same direction we were. We slightly accelerated our pace, walked off the bridge, and disappeared among the houses. Later on, we were told that the Nazis searched for us on the bank of the river. If we had soaked our feet a couple of minutes longer, I would have never written these words.

After we reached the western suburbs of Koprzywnica and entered the farmyard where we had left our bicycles, we noticed an unusual activity in the neighborhood--hundreds of armed Cossacks, who served in the Nazi Army, were looking for overnight quarters. Some of them were on the way to our friend's farmyard. We rushed toward the entrance of the house. Our friend was calm and directed us to the attic. As soon as we had climbed the steps to the attic and closed the trap door, a group of Cossacks entered the house and decided to stay there. Hoping that the Cossacks would leave the house for a moment, we waited--in vain--for a couple of hours. The Cossacks fed their horses in the yard, fixed a dinner for themselves, and ate and drank for hours. We didn't know what to do. Finally, the farmer came up to the attic and told us that the soldiers had enough whiskey to drink that we could safely come down, take our bicycles, and go. He gave us some baskets to carry to the barn and told us to pretend we were members of the family. We followed his instructions and got away safely from the midst of the Cossacks. We were very lucky. Now, after forty-seven years, I was describing the above events to my family.

Soon my family and I left Koprzywnica and drove toward Sandomierz. On both sides of the highway we saw beautifully kept orchards and new brick houses in their midst. Even though I knew the area very well, I could not recognize the villages along the highway. Their names were the same, but the villages and houses had changed. I drove the car as slowly as I could to take in everything that I saw.

When we came to the village of Samborzec, I looked for the grain mill which during my youth belonged to Mr. Misiuda. Finally, I noticed the mill, which appeared much smaller. However, I did not see the Misiudas' residence, which I remembered so well because in it four of my friends and I disarmed a group of vicious Nazis. One of them was a notorious high-ranking officer of the S.D. whose name was Schultz. He and his associates were responsible for the torture and death of many Polish patriots.

The Nazis arrived at the Misiudas' residence unannounced and demanded schnapps and food. They were armed with automatic and semiautomatic weapons. Mr. and Mrs. Misiuda were forced to be hospitable. They offered them food and drinks.

When the five of us approached the Misiuda residence, the Nazis were in the dining room. Two of us took positions outside the residence, and three of us, myself included, went in with pistols ready to fire. The Nazis were at the table eating and drinking. They were totally surprised to see us. We asked them to get up slowly and raise their hands. All of them obeyed our order with the exception of one whose hand went toward his pocket. One of my friends fired and wounded him in the arm.The wounded Nazi had an attack of hysteria. While two of my friends kept their guns aimed at the Nazis, I went around the table, searched them, and collected their weapons. The wounded Nazi had a pistol in his pocket. I had to calm his hysteria before I searched him and took the weapon from him. One of the weapons which I took from the Germans was a very modern and brand-new submachine gun with alot of ammunition. Before we left, we disconnected the telephones and disabled the Nazis' car. Then we disappeared into the countryside.

As we traveled through the village of Samborzec, I narrated the dramatic occurrence to my family. Soon we were in the city of Sandomierz, which was founded in pre-Christian times. The city was built on a hill overlooking the Vistula River.

While approaching the city, I noticed that the suburban area had increased considerably. The suburban fields and orchards gave way to new housing developments. In the thirty-three years of my absence, the city had doubled its size.

The first building which appeared before us in the downtown area was the medieval castle which hangs on the side of the hill. Before World War II, the Polish authorities used the ancient castle as a maximum security prison. After the Nazis occupied Poland in 1939, they, too, used it as a prison. Following World War II,the Polish Communist regime, in its initial stage, also kept prisoners in the castle. When I left Poland in 1957, a Communist prison was still in the historic castle. Now, as we came up the hill to the castle's main gate, we discovered that the castle had been converted to a regional museum. We parked our car and entered the castle.

After buying tickets, we began visiting it. We were very impressed by the professional restoration of the interior of the castle. The administration of the museum had collected many valuable objects of antiquity and regional art. In one of the rooms we found a portrait of Olga Bogdanska (1865-1940), a relative of mine on the side of my paternal grandmother. The oil painting was executed by a well-known artist. Our sons spent most of the time in the hall where the ancient weapons and armor were.

Before we ended our visit, I took my family to the western side of the castle and told them that in the middle of February in 1944, I took an active part in an attempt to release political prisoners whom the Nazis kept in the castle. I showed them the western slope of the hill by which a group of friends and I approached the castle. This is what happened.

## Chapter IX

According to my best knowledge, our intelligence service notified the leadership of our guerrilla group that the Nazis had imprisoned in the castle a number of Polish Home Army officers they had arrested in Cracow. These officers were about to be transferred to one of the extermination camps. There was no time to waste.

Our secret service established contact with one of the Polish prison guards whose own son was one of the political prisoners. He gave our secret service men the layout of the prison cells in the castle and told them that every day at 4:30 a.m. he and a couple of other guards came out of the castle on its western side to feed a few hogs and a dog in the yard. One of the guards always carried the keys to the prison cells. in such a situation, seizing the three guards, entering the castle, and releasing the political prisoners appeared very easy.

Full of confidence, our group left the manor of Zlota shortly after midnight and approached the castle from the west. We hid the sleighs and horses in the suburbs and walked the rest of the way. By the time we approached the castle and took our assigned positions, an auxiliary unit was already placed in the downtown area to protect us from the Nazi police stationed there and from the soldiers who were in a nearby base. It appears to me that the members of that group cut the telephone line which went to the castle.

To the best of my recollection, I was assigned to a small group of men who were to climb the western side of the castle hill, enter the yard, and seize the guards. As the time came to start our action, we began to climb the hill. There was snow under our feet and the freezing weather made our hands stick to the steel of our weapons. We walked up slowly and quietly. Most of the lights outside the prison were turned off. Once we reached the fence, which was made of boards, we began to work on a couple of weak boards. After a while, one of them gave in. Slowly and noiselessly, we removed another board. The opening in the fence was large enough for us to enter the yard one by one.

As soon as we entered the yard where the pigsty and doghouse were, the dog, which was quiet until then, began to bark. At the same time, a small light went on in the interior stairway as the guards came down to feed the animals.We froze for a moment and waited for them to come out into the yard. If I am not mistaken, they came down the steps about halfway, and one of them hearing the barking of the dog, looked through the window and noticed us. All of a sudden, the spotlights went on and one of the guards opened a window and fired at us. We had no explosives on us to blow up the door, so we cautiously, one after the other, left the yard through the hole in the fence and returned to the base of the hill. Once there, we began to fire at the windows of the stairway. Our guards on the sides of the castle opened fire also. At the same time, the auxiliary group in the center of the city began to fire at the bank building and the building in which the Nazi police were stationed. Soon, German flares appeared in the sky. By that time, we had begun to pull out towards our sleighs. Moments later, we were speeding along the Vistula River into the security of the countryside.

A few days after our unsuccessful attempt to free the prisoners, we learned that the Polish prison guard--named Marchewka--who had collaborated with us got drunk and notified the other guards, who served the Nazis, about our intentions. The other guards did not entirely believe him but nevertheless were very cautious. That is why the barking of the dog alerted the guards and made them turn on the spotlights--in the light of which they noticed us and the opening in the fence.

As my family and I left the old castle and began walking toward the parking lot, we stopped for a moment to take another look at the impressive castle. At that time, I had a recollection of a very unusual historical event which took place in the courtyard of the castle. It happened during the second half of the seventeenth century. The Swedish Wars were coming to an end and the Poles were rapidly expelling the enemy troops from their country. The city of Sandomierz and its castle were still in the hands of the Swedish Army. The Poles attacked the Swedes and forced them to abandon the city and the castle. Shortly before they left, the Swedes mined a part of the castle where a large quanitiy of gunpowder was stored. A patrol of Polish cavalry entered the courtyard of the castle as soon as the Swedes left. A powerful explosion shook the castle hill. The cavalrymen were all killed with the exception of one, who, along with his horse, was lifted into the air by the explosion and carried safely across the Vistula River to the opposite bank. Neither the man nor his horse suffered any physical harm.

## Chapter IX

Soon, we drove up the hill to visit the Cathedral of Blessed Virgin Mary, which was built in Gothic sytle in 1360. This beautiful church, which can accommodate about four thousand people, replaced the original Romanesque church which was constructed in the second half of the tenth century.

Before we entered the cathedral, we walked to the southeastern side of the churchyard to see, from a considerable elevation, the Vistula River, the castle, St. James Church, and the medieval granary.

St. James Church and the monastery adjacent to it were constructed by a group of Dominican monks in 1226. When I was looking at the church, I was reminded that during the Mongolian invasion of Poland in 1241, the city of Sandomierz fell and most of the citizens lost their lives at the hands of the barbarians. The Dominican monks were praying in the church when a band of Mongolians entered it. There were forty monks in the church at the time. The Mongolians killed them all with the exception of one monk who managed to hide in the choir. From his hiding place, he witnessed the living faith with which his fellow monks were dying and was edified by what he saw. Soon he came out from his hiding place and joined his brethren in their martyrdom.

From the churchyard, we went into the cathedral to pray and to visit it. As soon as we entered the church, I was amazed to see that its interior had not changed at all. After it was restored following World War II, it remained in excellent condition.

Before giving a guided tour of the church to my wife and our sons, I asked them to follow me to the sanctuary. There we knelt and prayed. During the prayer, I had trouble concentrating. My mind was full of memories. As a young seminarian, I took part in the services of this church for six years. Toward the end of the sixth year of my theological studies, I received here the orders of the deaconate and the priesthood. A few years after my priestly ordination, my bishop assigned me to preach in this ancient church.

After we finished our prayers, I asked my family to look at the walls of the sanctuary and see the beautiful Byzantine frescoes which are some of the most beautiful paintings of this kind in Poland. They were accidentally discovered when a large piece of plaster fell off during artillery fire at the beginning of

World War II.

From the sanctuary, we went to the side naves of the cathedral to view very large oil paintings which are placed in panels on the walls. They represent the most important events in the history of the city of Sandomierz. Most of the pictures depict the atrocities committed by the Mongolians on the citizens of Sandomierz. The martyrdom of the Dominican Monks in St. James Church is well-represented by the artist.

There is also a large picture which portrays a very tragic event which took place during one of the Mongolian invasions. The city of Sandomierz survived the Mongolian siege at that time because the young daughter of the Castellan of Sandomierz sacrificed her life to save the city. She coordinated her heroic act with the defenders of the city and then went to the leader of the Mongolian horde and told him that if he would spare her life, in return she would lead him and his men through a secret tunnel into the city of Sandomierz. The leader of the barbarians agreed. She led the enemies into a long dead-end tunnel which the water of the Vistula River had made in the limestone hill. When all of the Mongolians had entered the tunnel, the defenders of the city blocked the entrance with stones and mortar. Soon the Mongolians realized what had happened and murdered the heroine, but they also died in the tunnel. The citizens of Sandomierz were saved.

Most of the paintings depict the oriental cruelty with which the Mongolians inflicted death on the people of Sandomierz in 1226 or on other occasions whenever they managed to breach the defensive walls.

According to the records of the cathedral, the canons of the collegiate chapter commissioned the painting of all these historic pictures. A couple of canons were dishonest in paying the painters, so the artist took revenge on them by portraying them in the pictures as cruel Mongolians. The artist's revenge was discovered some time after the pictures were already completed and placed in the panels.

Following our visit to the cathedral, we walked to see the House of Jan Dlugosz (1415-1480), a famous historian who in his younger days was a canon of the Collegiate Church in Sandomierz. The house, built of brick, is very well-preserved. During my seminary days, my professor of liturgy lived in the old house. There was also a small museum in it.

## Chapter IX

From the House of Jan Dlugosz, we went to the market square, which is in the center of the old city. In the middle of the market square there is a well-preserved medieval town hall. We spent some time admiring the architecture of the town hall and other ancient buildings which were symmetrically constructed on the four sides of the town hall.

After viewing the town hall, we walked toward the Opatowska Gate, which was a part of the ancient defensive walls. Then we went to see the campus of the Diocesan Seminary of Sandomierz. I wanted my family to see the place where I spent ten very exciting years of my life; six years as a student and four years as an administrator.

The seminary buildings had not changed much, although their external appearance had deteriorated to some extent. St. Michael's Church, which is a part of the seminary campus, appeared to be well-kept, but its doors were locked.

As we stopped for a moment in front of the church and the main seminary building, I explained to my family that both were originally constructed for a group of Benedictine nuns who came to Sandomierz a long time ago. The Benedictine Abbey was built in late medieval times and St. Michael's Church was added in 1632. The church has very interesting beginnings. The money for its construction was donated by a very rich lawyer from Warsaw who as a poor youth depended on the charity of the Benedictine nuns in Sandomierz. He was a student in the Jesuit College for Nobility which was located about a quarter of a mile from the abbey.

The Jesuits built their college at the end of the sixteenth century to educate the sons of well-to-do nobility, but from time to time some poor-but-capable young men enrolled in this institution of higher learning. Such poor students were given meals by wealthy families and charitable institutions. Since the Benedictine Abbey was known for its charity, some of the poor students used to come to the abbey's kitchen to receive food. Some students ate there; others came with pails to take meals to their quarters.

One of the students who carried his meals from the kitchen to his quarters studied law and became an outstanding lawyer. As such, he became very wealthy. However, he never forgot the poverty of his college years and the generosity of the

Benedictine nuns. One day he returned to Sandomierz to express his gratitude to the nuns. He brought with him the pail in which he used to carry his meals. This time however, the pail was full of gold coins, which he offered as a gift to the mother abbess for the needs of the abbey. Since the mother abbess felt that a church was needed more than anything else, the gift of gold was used for the construction of St. Michael's Church.

The Benedictine nuns occupied the abbey and used the church until the end of the last century, when the government of Russia, which occupied this part of Poland, prohibited the abbey from accepting young ladies as candidates for the sisterhood. As a result of this prohibition, the population of the abbey grew smaller and smaller. Finally, when only two old nuns remained, the Russian authorities seized the buildings for the use of the state. Sometime thereafter, the Russian authorities expressed an interest in exchanging the Benedictine property for a downtown multistory building which housed the diocesan seminary. The church authorities saw many advantages in such an exchange and agreed to it. Thus, the Benedictine Abbey was converted into the seminary building. Years after the exchange, a new wing was added to the existing structure.

When my family and I entered the campus of the Diocesan Seminary, we were struck by the lack of activity. At first, I attributed this to the fact that the seminarians were away from the campus during summer vacation. Then I reflected for a moment and came to the conclusion that even if the seminarians were gone for the summer, the employees of the institution should have been involved in some activities. I was puzzled and did not know what to think. After a while, somebody came by and explained to me that the Diocesan Seminary was no longer in Sandomierz. The institution was moved recently to the city of Radom, which is the largest city in the diocese and is centrally located. The diocesan bishop and his administrative offices were also in the process of moving to the same city. This bit of information solved my puzzle.*

As we looked at the lifeless campus, many memories rushed into my mind. I could almost visualize the excitement of my first day in the seminary as a student at the end of August in

*Later on, I discovered that the Diocese of Sandomierz was divided in two: the Diocese of Sandomierz & the Diocese of Radom.

1946; the faces of my classmates; our professors, studies, and exams; prayers and meditations in the chapel; friendships and teamwork in choir and liturgy; joyful celebrations of important feats and ordinations; struggle on the way of holiness; dreams of successful ministry and Christian martyrdom; successes or failures; and many other youthful experiences. Memories of my work as an administrator came also to mind. I thought about my predecessor, Father Stefan Siedlecki, whom the agents of the Communist government imprisoned for doing his best to keep the seminary open in spite of Stalin's violent persecution of the church. I remembered the early days of my work at the seminary and the very warm reception by the faculty members who, with very few exceptions, were my former professors. I thought about the struggle with the Communist authorities who decided that all theological seminaries should be taxed to destroy their economic base and force them to close. I remembered surveillance, interrogations, and intimidation by the all-powerful secret police. As I recollected all these things, I looked around, by the power of old habit, to see if the agents of the secret police still watched my activities. Old habits die very slowly.

From the seminary campus, we walked to a nearby building where I was involved in disarming a group of Nazi pilots in November of 1943. As we stopped in front of the three-story building, I narrated, for the benefit of my family, the dramatic sequence of events which took place in this building in the middle of November 1943. At that time, the Nazi empire was still very powerful. In Sandomierz, many German military units were stationed in various parts of the city. The streets of the city were continuously patrolled by military police. This gave the military personnel a feeling of security. Being aware of this situation, the regional superiors of the underground Home Army ordered our guerrilla unit to take over the three-story building at 18 Mickiewicza Street and disarm a group of pilotes *(Luftwaffe)* and some railroad police *(Bahnschutzpolizei)* who were stationed there.

The underground intelligence service provided the commanding officer of our unit, Captain "Kaktus", with a detailed floor plan of each story in the building, a fairly good description of the occupants of various rooms, and the location of the military supplies.

On Friday, November 12, 1943, after disarming the German guard, we entered the building and successfully disarmed about fifty Germans.

After recollecting the experience of disarming the German pilots and railroad police in the three-story building, I led my family to St. Joseph's Church, which borders the city park. The church was built in the second part of the seventeenth century and there is nothing unusual about its architecture. What is unusual about St. Joseph's Church is the former pastor who served the church in the early part of World War II and suffered Christian martyrdom for the sake of truth. The ashes from his cremated body were sealed in a wall of the sanctuary. I wanted us to visit the church and thank God for the life and the calling of a great priest, Father Antoni Rewera.

After we entered the church and approached the sanctuary, I told my family about the following events which took place in the final period of Father Rewera's life.

Nazi policemen stopped the priest on the street in Sandomierz. They asked him for his identification card and subjected him to a personal search. During the search, they found on him a copy of a Polish underground newspaper. They arrested him. During interrogation, the Nazis asked the priest whether he knew the person who gave him the copy of the underground paper. Father Rewera replied that he did, indeed, know the person. The interrogators asked for the name of the person. Father Rewera refused to divulge the name, saying to the Nazis that if he gave them the name of the person they would imprison and possibly kill that person. The Nazis were disappointed but had a great deal of respect and sympathy for the elderly priest. One of them confidentially approached Bishop Jan Lorek and suggested that if Father Rewera would change his story and say in subsequent interrogations that he no longer remembered the name of the person who had handed him the newspaper, he could be released from prison; otherwise, he might end up in Auschwitz. The bishop sent a message to the prisoner which suggested the change of story. Father Rewera rejected the suggestion and said, "All my life I spoke nothing but truth. How can I lie in my old age?"

The prediction of the sympathetic Nazi interrogator came true. Father Rewera was sent to Auschwitz, where, to the end of his life, he ministered to fellow priests and laymen.

Chapter IX

After he died and his body was cremated, a mailman delivered a small package to the parish office. In it were the ashes of the priest. The parishioners of St. Joseph's Church decided to place the ashes in the left wall of the sanctuary. When the war ended, they also placed a plaque with an inscription which read something like this: "Here are the ashes of our dear pastor, Father Rewera, the Martyr of Truth."

As soon as I finished talking about Father Rewera, a large group of teenagers under the leadership of a young seminarian entered the church for prayers and instruction. My family and I knelt down and prayed before leaving. After we left St. Joseph's Church, we drove toward the military base which was located northwest of Sandomierz on the road which led to the city of Opatow. As we came close to the base, I recollected a couple of events from my teen years.

The first event took place in the spring of 1938. At that time, I was about to graduate from the public grade school and I became interested in the Air Force Academy. In order to apply for the academy, I needed a health certificate from a military physician attached to the base of the Second Regiment of Infantry in Sandomierz. I will never forget the day my classmate, Kazimierz Deren, and I walked all the way from Sulislawice to Sandomierz for our physical examinations. The weather on that day was very beautiful and our hopes were high. When we reached the military base, the soldiers in the guardhouse directed us to the base's infirmary, where the physicians had their offices. As we waited for our examinations, a couple of medics engaged us in conversation and wanted to know why we were eager to enroll in the Air Force Academy and eventually serve as pilots in the Polish Air Force. They were convinced that military service was not a bed of roses and that serving in the air force was more dangerous than serving in the army or navy.

Before we were able to answer their questions, a nurse came and asked us to get ready for our physical examinations. We handed her the forms which had been mailed to us by the academy, and soon we individually underwent our physical examinations. After we put our clothes on, the physician announced the results: my friend failed but I passed with flying colors. I felt happy that my health was good but my happiness was marred by my friend's disappointment. I did everything possible to control my happiness while I tried to console Kazimierz.

The second event of my teen years which I recollected occurred on the morning of September 1, 1939, the day Nazi Germany attacked Poland. Early in the morning on that memorable day, a couple of fifth column Nazis stirred the people in our town at about 4:00 a.m., saying that a unit of German tanks appeared already near Staszow. They told the people that the Germans would be forcing young men and teenage boys into their service.

My first cousin, Jan Mazgaj, his friend, Waclaw Kos, and I decided to go immediately to the base of the Second Regimental Infantry in Sandomierz and volunteer for service. After packing some provisions,we walked from Jeziory to Sandomierz. But when we arrived at the base, a couple of guards at the gate told us that the Second Regiment was already on its way to the front. They advised us to cross the Vistula River and proceed east, where we might have a chance to join some infantry unit. We took their advice seriously and walked toward the eatern border of Poland for a couple of weeks, but every military unit which we came across refused to take us for lack of weapons and ammunition.

After viewing the military base, my family and I drove by the soccer stadium, which reminded me of my friend "Bobo" (Zbigniew Kabata) and his companion "Fala" (Janusz Lipski), who carried out the execution of a death sentence on the person of Zygmunt Gaszynski, a notorious Gestapo agent. Gestapo transferred Gaszynski from Radom to Sandomierz with an order to destroy the network of Home Army in the District of Sandomierz. For his perfidious activities both in Radom and Sandomierz, the military tribunal of Home Army condemned Gaszynski to death. Since he was a very clever and cautious man, underground soldiers failed to carry out the sentence on numerous occasions. Finally "Bobo" and "Fala" volunteered to terminate the harmful activities of the Gestapo agent.

According to "Bobo's" account,* the stalking of the agent was a very grueling task. One time "Bobo"and "Fala" encoun-

*I refer here to "Bobo's" oral account, but most of all to his written account. For the written account, see Zbigniew Kabata "Bobo", *Wiersze* (Poems), (Wroclaw: Wroclawskie Zaklady Graficzne 1993), pp. 49-55.

tered him but had some doubts about his identity so they did not shoot him. After that encounter, they did not spot him for a long time. From time to time, they felt very discouraged. At such times, they thought about forcing their way into the agent's apartment and holding his wife at gunpoint until he returned home. This plan, however, had a serious disadvantage because the agent's apartment was very close to the military barracks and next door to the quarters of German officers.

In the meantime, the underground intelligence service became aware that Gaszynski would be one of the players in an upcoming soccer game. It was Saturday when "Bobo" and "Fala" were informed of this new development. The soccer game was scheduled for the following day, Sunday, October 24, 1943. A member of the underground intelligence service was assigned to meet "Bobo" and "Fala" near the stadium, lead them to it, and cautiously point our Gaszynski to them. The stadium where the game was to be held was about three hundred meters from the military base. "Bobo" and "Fala" spent the rest of the day Saturday and Sunday morning on preparations and waiting for their dramatic performance at the stadium. "Bobo" confessed that the preparation was not a problem but the long hours of waiting was a nerve-shattering experience for him and his companion.

Finally, the time of retribution had come. "Bobo" and "Fala" met their contact near a red house. For better identification, the contact wore a gray topcoat and navy blue hat. From the red house, "Bobo" and "Fala" followed him at a certain distance. Since soccer games were very rare during the war, there were crowds of people on the way to the stadium. Hundreds of them wore military uniforms and were armed with pistols.

As they reached the periphery of the stadium, "Bobo" and "Fala" could hear the kicking of the ball and the shouting of the fans. A few moments later, they were near enough to see the individual players. But which of them was Gaszynski? According to the characterization of Gaszynski given to them by intelligence service, he was supposed to be tall and very well-built with black curly hair and a long nose. As "Bobo" and "Fala" concentrated their attention on every moving player, it appeared to them that there were two players who fit the characterization of Gaszynski. Their contact man, in his gray topcoat and navy blue hat, must have sensed their puzzlement, because he shouted, "Bravo Gaszynski, good kick!" From that time on, "Bobo" and

"Fala" kept their eyes on that player.

Having solved the problem of identification of the agent, "Bobo" and "Fala" had a bigger problem to solve. Namely, how to approach and shoot him in the middle of the stadium and other soccer players. When the solution to this problem appeared to be next to impossible, two long sounds of a whistle pierced the air and immediately the players stopped the game. It was intermission time. This gave the players a chance to have some refreshments which their family members or friends kept ready for them. The players gathered together in small groups to share comments about the game, and their relatives or friends began to approach and offer them refreshments or snacks. "Bobo" and "Fala" could not have asked for a better opportunity to execute the death sentence on the Gestapo operative. "Let's go," said "Bobo" to "Fala", and they went toward the group of players where Gaszynski was. Due to his size, Gaszynski towered over the others in the group.

As "Bobo" and "Fala" neared the group, Gaszynski's wife, a lanky blond, approached the group from another side and threw toward her husband, over the heads of his companions, a box of snacks. He opened it and began to offer apples to the others around him. "Bobo" and "Fala" approached the group and began to elbow their way toward Gaszynski. While "Fala" was fumbling for the pistol in his pocket, "Bobo" led the way.

After a few moments, "Bobo" was near the Nazi agent and there was no one between them. "Bobo" pulled out his pistol, aimed, and fired two times into the powerful body of Gaszynski. The shots appeared to be deadly. The Gestapo agent's body fell to the ground face-down. "Fala" fired two more shots into the agent's head. Pandemonium broke out. People were running away from the scene of the shooting. There was a great panic, not only among the civilians, but also among the military men. It was the best time for "Bobo" and "Fala" to take to their feet.

As "Bobo" started to run toward the fence which separated the residential area from the stadium, somebody fired at him a couple of times but missed. When "Fala" noticed that a German was pulling out his pistol, he fired at him just in time. As they dashed toward the fence, "Fala", with pistol in hand, ordered the people out of the way by shouting in German *raus, raus!*

## Chapter IX

When they were almost at the fence, they noticed a group of confused Germans near it. It was too late to avoid the group. So they pointed their pistols toward the Germans and shouted *weg!* at the top of their voices. The Germans obeyed the order with great speed. One of them, however, lost his cool and, in anticipation of being shot, covered his face with the palms of his hands.

In a few seconds, "Bobo" and "Fala" were already on the other side of the fence. Now they had to cross a small field as fast as possible. As they ran across the field, a German light machine gun opened up from a window of a nearby building. The bullets missed them. Then a determined German began to follow them with a gun in his hand. "Fala" noticed him, aimed and fired, but missed. He took aim again and fired. This time, the German fell to the ground.

After a moment of accelerated running, they reached the first suburan houses which provided a modicum of safety and protection. Some people were already there rushing through the gates in the orchard fences or scaling the fences. "Bobo" and "Fala" were too much in a hurry to follow others. They kicked out a couple of pickets in the fence and went through the opening. As they overcame the hurdles, they entered the field which led to safety. Soon "Bobo" and "Fala" were out of the reach of the Germans who might have followed them. They reloaded their magazines and then hugged and congratulated each other on the successful elimination of another dangerous Gestapo agent.

When the Soviet troops occupied Poland toward the end of World War II, "Bobo" managed to avaoid detention by the Communist authorities. He took refuge in Italy and joined the Polish Army, which still fought the Nazis under the command of General Anders.

At the end of the war, "Bobo" went to England, where he completed his undergraduate and graduate studies. After earning his doctorates in philosophy and marine biology, "Bobo" worked in the marine laboratory in Aberdeen for twelve years. As the result of his numerous scientific publications, "Bobo" was appointed to the professorship of Simon Fraser Burnaby University in British Columbia.

Soon we were on the way to the town of Nadbrzezie. We decided to drive back to our hotel in Polaniec via Tarnobrzeg. As we approached the bridge to cross the Vistula River, all of a sudden I remembered the day during the war when my friend, Jan Osemlak, and I rode a horse-driven cab to the other side of the river. The bridge then was carefully guarded by the Nazis. Two troopers armed with rifles and pistols stood guard on both ends of the bridge. From time to time they checked identification cards of the people who were on their way to the railroad station in the town of Nadbrzezie. We, too, were on the way to Nadbrzezie, where we were to disarm three Nazis who carried submachine guns. They were an escort assigned to protect a Polish bank official who carried two small suitcases full of cash.

The cabman who was to take us over the bridge to the town of Nadbrzezie was a member of our organization and fully realized the danger to which he was exposing himself. To my best recollection, he met us on the side street near St. Paul's Church in Sandomierz. As soon as we got in the back seat of the cab, he covered our legs with a lap cover. We put our right hands, with pistols ready to fire, under the cover. All three of us were tense and spoke very little.

Shortly, we were on the main road leading to the bridge. From a distance, we saw the guard booths on each side of the bridge. Soon, we were at the entrance to the bridge. The cabman slowed his horse. The guards looked at us with their searching eyes but did not stop us.

The road toward the railroad station in Nadbrzezie was very busy. Civilians and uniformed Germans were rushing toward the railroad station. As we came near to the section of the road where the disarmament of the Nazis was to take place, we let the cabman go back to Sandomierz. As soon as he left, we walked slowly toward the railroad station. Our timing appeared to be good. The Germans were very punctual, and we expected them to be in our section of the road any time. But when we looked behind us, we did not see them. To our great disappointment, they were a considerable distance ahead of us. In order to catch up with them, we quickened our pace.

By the time we came close to them, the Nazis were already near the railroad station. The presence of many uniformed Germans at the station made it impossible for us to disarm the escort. We were terribly frustrated and decided to return to Sandomierz. Soon our friends in Nadbrzezie hired a cabman who took us over the bridge without incident. As we were riding back to Sandomierz, we made plans to return to Nadbrzezie the following week to do what we had failed to do this time.

By the time I finished my World War II recollections, my family and I were nearing the city of Tarnobrzeg, where we intended to visit my youngest brother, Zbigniew.

Soon we were in the city. This time, my brother and his wife were home.We had a very enjoyable visit. Zbigniew had tears in his eyes when he saw me after thirty-three years. He was a little boy when I left Poland and we knew each other only from pictures. During the visit, we attempted to get acquainted as much as possible. We talked for a long time about our lives and families. Almost everything which he said I translated into English for the benefit of my wife and our sons. It was late in the evening when we said goodbye to Zbigniew and his wife and mother-in-law. From Tarnobrzeg, we drove to Loniow and then proceeded to our hotel in Polaniec to rest after a long and busy day.

# Chapter X

On Thursday, June 28, we visited our relatives in Polaniec and tried to learn as much as possible about our family's history. One of our relatives who is a retired teacher gave us a great deal of information which had been handed down to her by her father.

After visiting with our relatives, we went to the parish church and then did some shopping in local stores. We had no trouble buying bread and meat, but we were unable to get eggs.

In the afternoon, we drove to Gieraszowice to see my sister Danuta and her husband. When we arrived at their residence, their daughter Beata greeted us and told us that her parents were picking strawberries in the field behind the barn. While my wife and our sons were entertained by Beata, I walked to the field where my sister and her husband worked. On my way, I had to cross a road which I walked in my youth so many times to the city of Klimontow. As I crossed the dirt road, I was struck by its neglected condition. A new highway had been built to Klimontow, and the old road, which in my memory was rather wide and well-known, appeared before me narrow and forgotten. A very uneasy feeling came upon me as I crossed the road on the way to the strawberry field. I could not explain the feeling of uneasiness at first. Then, after reflecting for a moment, I realized the source of my uneasiness. It was a terrible real life drama whcih was staged before my youthful eyes by the Nazi SS units on the twenty-ninth day of October 1942, in the city of Klimontow.

On that memorable day, I walked this road to Klimontow in the company of a couple of my childhood friends to buy some things for my parents. It was early in the morning and many people were walking and riding on the road. They anticipated buying or selling things at the farmer's market which was to be held in Klimontow on that day. The city was a business paradise. Like most of the cities in the area, it was inhabited by a Jewish population. It appears to me that ninety percent of the people in Klimontow were Jewish. Most of them were store keepers; some were tailors and shoemakers; a few of them were lawyers and physicians.

In the early part of World War II, the Jewish population of the city doubled when the Nazis transported thousands of Jews from Vienna, Austria, to Klimontow. The Jews from Vienna differed from the local Jews. They dressed according to West European fashion and spoke German rather than Yiddish. They were well-educated, cultured, cosmopolitan, and wealthier than the Jews of Klimontow.

Shortly after they settled in the city of Klimontow, the Nazis forced all the Jews in the city to get organized and elect a so-called Jewish Council which was responsible for the affairs of the Jewish community. Soon the Nazis requested that Jewish work crews be sent daily to sweep the streets of the city, clean public bathrooms, and repair roads. Then, at the beginning of 1942, the Nazis told the Jewish Council that the time had come for the "resettlement" of Klimontow's Jewish population to Auschwitz. The Jews were terror-stricken. The Jewish Council began to negotiate with the Nazis about a postponement of the "resettlement". The Nazis agreed to postpone it under the condition that the Jews of Klimontow would give them so many pounds of gold.

The council agreed and the collection of gold began. After the gold was given to the Nazis, the Nazis were pleased and the Jews were hopeful. A couple of months later, the Nazis confronted the Jewish Council with a new demand for gold. Again, gold was collected and delivered to the Nazi authorities. Needless to say, the demands for gold and other precious metals were repeated again until the Jews had given everything they had. At that point, the Jews began to lose hope. From day to day, they expected to be "resettled" to Auschwitz.

The day my childhood friends and I walked the dirt road to Klimontow was the day of "resettlement," but we and the other people going to the city that day were not aware of it. When we walked through the Klimontow Forest toward its edge, we heard machine gun, submachine gun, and rifle fire coming from the direction of the city. Soon we noticed groups of people returning from Klimontow. They were frightened and nervous and told everybody on the road that the city of Klimontow was surrounded by SS troopers and the Jews were being herded into the market. The Jews who attempted to escape into the countryside were shot by troopers. The people who told us what was happening in Klimontow had not entered the city but observed from a distance. They advised us not to go any further but to return home. Most of the people on the road followed the advice. My friends and I decided to walk as close to the city as possible to see the tragic events.

Walking with an accelerated pace, we reached the edge of the forest and approached the Jewish cemetery which was in the fields outside the city. From the vicinity of the cemetery, we had an excellent view. Klimontow was below us. From that perspective, we saw the cordon of Nazi troopers posted in the fields. We were also able to see a number of bodies of those who had attempted to escape in our direction and were shot. We saw troopers herd groups of people at the end of Osiecka Street. Then we did not see anything until about 11:00 a.m., when we noticed a column of Jewish people, guarded by troopers, emerge at the end of Sandomierska Street. They were being led toward Nadbrzezie Railroad Station near Sandomierz. Most of the people carried suitcases or bags with their most valuable and necessary belongings. Everything else was left behind. Those of the Jewish people who could not keep pace with the marching column because they carried too many belongings or because of physical weakness were shot and left on the side of the road.

As soon, as the long column of the Jewish people of Klimontow disappeared from our sight, we ventured into the city, which had become a ghost town. The city, which was always alive and noisy, was as quiet as a cemetery. The sidewalks and streets were littered with Jewish corpses and stained with blood. There were also some non-Jewish corpses there. Obviously, some farm people from neighboring villages had entered the city in the early morning and were trapped there.

When we walked to the market, we saw some Polish policemen patrolling the city. They did not object to our presence. They ignored us. I am sure they were ashamed to serve the Nazis and be a part of the criminal, barbaric, shameful acts of their masters.

After walking around the market, we lost interest in any further exploration of the bloody scene of murder of innocent and helpless people. We decided to return home as soon as possible to tell our families what we had seen. After telling our parents, neighbors, and friends about our experience in Klimontow, we attempted to forget the whole thing. In my case, I never managed to forget it. So many things remind me of the human tragedy in the city of Klimontow: the simple sight of the dirt road behind my sister's barn called it to my mind after forty-eight long years.

In the summer of 1951, I did some research in the archives of the parish church in Klimontow, where I found very important information about a Jewish physician, Dr. Kaplan, who marched in the column of people from Klimontow to the railroad station in Nadbrzezie, the column of the Jewish people which my friends and I saw October 29, 1942.

According to this information, recorded by the pastor of the church, Dr. Kaplan was an excellent physician and a great human being. His patients, both Jewish and Christian, loved and respected him, not only for the sake of his professional skill, but also for his genuine love of all the people whom he met in his office and outside his office. Poor people came to his office for medical help and always received it without charge. In most instances, he provided free medicine for them.

When the first rumors of the "resettlement" of the Jewish population of Klimontow began to spread, many Christian patients of Dr. Kaplan offered him and his family shelter in their homes. The altruistic physician was touched by his patients' love for him but did not accept the offer, saying, "I cannot leave my people, because now they need me more than ever before." He went with his people to the railroad station in Nadbrzezie and then to the extermination camp in Auschwitz. I have no doubt that both on the way to the camp and in the camp, Dr. Kaplan served his people as long as there was life in him. His altruism and the sacrifice of his own life for others should never be forgotten.

My recollections of the tragic events in Klimontow were interrupted by my sister Danuta, who was returning from the strawberry field. Her husband was still working in the field but was about to quit. She asked me to accompany her to the farmhouse.

Soon my sister's family and my family were sitting

around the dining room table, enjoying a tasty meal and pleasant conversation. I did not say a word to anybody about my unpleasant recollections.

In the evening, we returned to our hotel in Polaniec to rest well before our long trip to Radom, where my brother Alexander lives.

## Chapter XI

On Friday, June 29, we began our journey to the city of Radom to visit my brother Alexander and his family.

When we left Polaniec, the sky was clear and the air was already warm. After driving northwest for a while, our highway entered the Forest of Staszow. During my youth, the forest was very large; now it appeared rather small and devastated. Many memories rushed to my mind as we drove deeper and deeper into the forest. As a young boy, I walked through the forest on many occasions. Later on, as a soldier of the Polish Home Army, I crisscrossed it with others searching for shelter or for a proper place to ambush the Nazis who traveled quite frequently between Staszow and Sandomierz.

The old trees of the Forest of Staszow witnessed many life-and-death struggles between us, the natives of this land, and the Nazi foreigners who were far away from their homeland to enslave and exterminate us. Why did they leave their cities, town, villages, fields, and forests to rape and violate a neighboring country?

The Forest of Staszow witnessed also many crimes which the Nazi barbarians committed against humanity. The forest contains many individual and mass graves in which the Nazis who were stationed in the area buried their victims.

As we continued driving through the forest, I remembered that in the summer of 1952 I spent some time there for the last time before leaving for the United States.

Shortly after my ordination to the priesthood, I began one month of vacation at home and was looking forward to the free time with my family, relatives, and friends. Before I began to enjoy the vacation, the diocesan bishop, Jan Kanty Lorek, asked me to go to the Parish of Wisniowa near Staszow and take the place of the pastor, who had become ill and was hospitalized. I went to the parish immediately and began a very joyful month of ministry. Some of the parishioners lived on the edge of the Staszow Forest.

It appears to me, after thirty-nine years, that one of the parishioners of the Wisniowa parish took me to the forest and showed me a mass grave in which the Nazi criminals had buried a bride and groom, their parents, brothers, sisters, and relatives, and all the guests who attended the wedding feast. According to my best recollection, the parishioner told me that he witnessed the execution.

On the day of the execution, which took place very early in the morning, he was picking mushrooms in the forest when all of a sudden he heard the roar of trucks. He approached the area from which the noise of motors was coming and watched from a distance. The trucks pulled into a small clearing in the forest and stopped. Uniformed Nazis armed with submachine guns appeared on the scene and surrounded the clearing with weapons ready to fire. Soon, other Nazis brought from the trucks into the clearing groups of people, including a bride and groom in their wedding apparel.

The Nazis handed shovels to the people and ordered them to dig a mass grave. The digging began and after a while the grave was ready. The victims were then ordered to listen to the sentence which was read by the commanding officer. Following the reading of the sentence, the officer ritualistically washed his hands and commanded his subordinates to place the people on the edge of the mass grave. Once they were there, the officer commanded: Fire! Most of the victims fell into the grave, while others remained on the surface of the earth. Their bodies were pushed into the grave by the excited Nazis, who then covered the bodies with earth.

As soon as the burial was completed, the Nazis left the place of murder in a hurry. The witness of the atrocious crime waited until the noise of the motors died out. Then he went to see the grave. There was human blood everywhere near the grave. He had the impression that the fresh earth on the mass grave moved in some areas. Perhaps it was just an illusion, or perhaps there was still some life left in some of the victims. He was frightened and bewildered. It was too much for him to remain in this place of horror any longer; he rushed home to share the bad and disturbing tidings with others.

A few days later, the witness of the hideous crime learned

that the people whom he saw executed by the Nazis had been brought from one of the villages near the city of Sandomierz, possibly on the eastern side of the Vistula River. Allegedly, a couple of drunk Nazi officers came uninvited to the wedding feast in the village. The people at the wedding treated the officers politely, hospitably, and offered them food. The officers were not interested in food, however, but in young ladies present at the wedding. When they began to act immodestly, chasing the girls, some young men attempted to stop them. This led to a physical struggle between the officers and the young men. The officers were subdued and forced out of the house. They left with threats of revenge. Before the people managed to leave the wedding feast, a group of Nazis arrived and arrested everybody. The people present at the wedding were accused of attacking and beating the Nazi officers. They were taken to a prison, interrogated, and condemned to death. They were taken to the Staszow Forest for execution; a very typical Nazi justice.

As soon as I finished my recollection of the tragic events which took place in the Staszow Forest, we entered the suburbs of the city of Staszow. The traffic was very light and the road full of curves. Downtown, we took a wrong turn and lost our road. This gave us a chance to see more of the city. Soon we found our road and were driving through beautiful fields, villages, and towns toward the city of Rakow. There were very few cars on the road. Many people walked or bicycled to neighboring towns or villages. It was the Feast of St. Peter and St. Paul the Apostles on that day, so the people were on their way to their parish churches for services.

Before we approached Rakow, I explained to my family that the city, although insignificant in appearance, played a very important role in the history of the Unitarian movement.

The Unitarians, who originated in western Europe during the early times of the Reformation, experienced persecution in France and Switzerland for their unorthodox beliefs. One of their leaders, Michael Servetus (1511-1553), was accused of heresy by John Calvin and put to death in Switzerland. Poland, which had very liberal laws toward religious beliefs and was spared the fanaticism of the Reformation, offered a refuge to the Unitarians. They came to Poland in great numbers and made the city of Rakow their center. They were known there as Arians or Socinians. Soon Rakow became the intellectual and spiritual center of the Unitarians, not only for Poland but for western civilization. Many very important religious books were published in Rakow and distributed from Rakow to various countries.* The Unitarians experienced a great success in Poland.

This great success was partially due to the fact that religious bigotry was always alien to the Polish people in general. For centuries, the Poles, who are mostly Roman Catholics, lived in peace and harmony with Orthodox Christians, Jews, and Mohammedans. Many Polish noblemen were accustomed to sending their sons to Switzerland and Germany to be educated in various universities. Having completed their studies abroad, they returned to Poland not only with a good education but also with a desire of ecclesiastical reformation. Some of these young noblemen converted to Calvinism or Lutheranism before they returned home.

One such nobleman, the owner of the town of Rakow, who was already a Calvinist, converted to Unitarianism in 1599. His name was Jacob Sienienski. He was persuaded to establish in Rakow a college and a printing press. Soon both of them had been established and were successful.

The success of the Unitarian movement in Rakow and in other cities in Poland caused great jealously among some of the Roman Catholic bishops. This narrow-minded jealously gave rise to thus far unknown religious bigotry. Due to this new bigotry, the Calvinist and Unitarian churches in Lublin were destroyed in 1627. At the instigation of Jacob Zadzik, bishop of Cracow, the Diet of Warsaw passed a law against the Unitarians of Rakow on May 1, 1638. Soon thereafter, members of the Jesuit Order advocated the banishing of the Unitarians from Poland. In 1658, the Diet of Warsaw decreed the banishment of the Unitarians in the whole country. Thus came to an end one of the finest religious and educational movements in Poland--the victim of narrow-mindedness, jealousy, and religious bigotry.

In downtown Rakow, we parked our car and went shopping. In one of the bakeries, we bought the most delicious bread

*For instance, *The Socian Racovian Catechism*, which was published in Rakow in 1605.

and hard rolls. We also went to a well-supplied delicatessen to buy some excellent smoked meat.

From Rakow, we drove toward the city of Kielce to visit my friend, Wlodzimierz Gruszczcynski, a fellow freedom fighter during World War II.

Near the city of Kielce, we found a large gasoline station which had unleaded gasoline. We were delighted with the discovery and filled our gasoline tank and the three containers in the trunk of our car.

Soon we were in the suburbs of Kielce. As we drove toward the downtown area, I began to recall my last visit to the city, a visit which I will never forget. According to my best recollection, it took place in the spring of 1955. I was working then in the Diocesan Major Seminary in Sandomierz. One day, very early in the morning, the doorkeeper of the seminary called me up and said there was an emergency and somebody wanted to see me immediately. I dressed in a hurry and went down to the parlor. A middle-aged lady waited for me. She was in tears. She told me that her teenage daughter was dying of an abdominal infection in the local hospital. The chief surgeon, who was also a Communist administrator of the hospital, told the mother there was nothing he could do for the dying teenager. The mother suggested a consultation with a well-know surgeon from Kielce. The chief surgeon refused to call the other surgeon, saying there was no use to bother--the girl was dying. The desperate mother asked me to bring the surgeon from Kielce as soon as possible. She believed he could save her daughter's life. She came to me because I had visited her daughter in the hospital and because I had a large English motorcycle.

I agreed to go immediately. It took me about three hours to reach Kielce. I was in the hospital at 7:00 a.m. Soon the well-known surgeon arrived in his office. His nurse introduced me to him. I explained the purpose of my visit. He agreed to go with me to Sandomierz and to perform surgery if necessary. I could see on his face and hear in his voice a great desire to save the young lady's life. We were of the same age and seemed to understand each other very well. As he was getting ready to ride with me, the hospital administrator came in and offered the surgeon the use of the hospital ambulance so that, if necessary, the patient could be brought to Kielce for surgery. The surgeon was very happy about this new development and accepted the favor with great joy. He went to Sandomierz in the ambulance while I returned by motorcycle.

On the way back to Sandomierz, I prayed for the life of the young patient and God's blessings on the surgeon. I felt a spirit of fulfillment in my heart and gratitude to the young surgeon.

After examining the patient, the surgeon decided to take her with him to the hospital in Kielce. There he performed a successful surgery and saved the life of the young lady. Everybody was happy except the Communist surgeon and administrator of the Holy Ghost Hospital in Sandomierz. He was furious because his prognosis did not come true and the young patient lived. His anger was directed at me and the young surgeon from Kielce. I do not know what he did to revenge himself on his colleague in the profession; in my case, he went to my bishop and accused me of interfering in his work at the hospital. Since, as a powerful Communist, he was feared by everybody, the bishop suggested that I apologize to him for the sake of peace. I did so reluctantly.

Years after I left Poland and was teaching undergraduates at Penn State University, a visitor from Poland came to the campus. She happened to be from Sandomierz. During a conversation about our mutual acquaintances, I asked her about the young lady who almost died of the abdominal infection. The visitor informed me that after graduating from college, the young lady went to medical school and became a physician. It is quite possible that she became a surgeon and now saves the lives of others.

Soon my family and I were in the center of the city of Kielce. We had very little trouble finding the residence of my friend. Unfortunately, no one was home. We were disappointed and decided to stop again on the way back from Radom. In the meantime, we resumed our journey to Radom.

On the way to Radom, we stopped at a roadside restaurant for lunch. It was a rather large and clean restaurant, operated as a cooperative. We enjoyed the excellent food which was served there. We took a table next to a window so we could see the traffic on the highway by which we came. On the other side of the highway there was a private residence. About thirty-five persons waited in line to enter it. We were puzzled. I asked our waitress what was going on there. She replied that the family that lived in the residence had opened up a bakery and baked the finest bread and rolls in the whole area. Soon we saw a truck full of sacks of flour pull into the driveway and a couple of men began to unload it. My wife, seeing all this, finished her lunch sooner than the rest of us and went to buy some bread and rolls in the home bakery. The baked goods were of an excellent quality. We admired the spirit of enterprise of the family which produced such fine baked goods.

Following lunch, we drove directly to Radom. We reached the city at about 3:00 p.m. Even though I had lived in Radom for six months, I was lost in its suburbs, which had developed beyond recognition. However, with very helpful directions given to us by a taxi driver, we had no trouble finding the apartment building in which my brother and his family live.

Soon we were at the door of my brother's apartment and ringing the doorbell. My sister-in-law answered the door. I had never met her before. I recognized her only from pictures. She was delighted to see us and asked us to come in. In a moment, my brother's son appeared. He was painting an adjacent apartment into which he had moved recently in anticipation of marriage. My brother had not returned yet from work. In the meantime, we became acquainted with my sister-in-law and nephew. They helped us to catch up with the most recent news in their lives. The family album full of pictures helped tremendously. We saw the baptisms, first Holy Communions, confirmations, weddings, and funerals--a panorama of our family life.

Before my sister-in-law finished cooking dinner, my brother Alexander returned home. He was apologetic about being late, explaining that a couple of friends from work had asked him to have a beer with them. We had a very emotional reunion. Olek, as we called him at home, was in his early teens when I left Poland. Now he and his wife have grownup children and some grandchildren. Two of their married daughters live a considerable distance from Radom.

During dinner and following dinner, we talked and talked, recollecting past events in our family life. It was wonderful to be together after so many years of being away. What a joyful family reunion!

It must have been about 6:00 p.m. when we left my

brother's apartment and began driving back toward Kielce. As we were leaving the city of Radom, I thought about the most wonderful experiences which I had during my six months of ministry in this great city.

My ministry in Radom occurred under most unusual conditions. In the summer of 1956, I resigned my post as an administrator of the seminary in Sandomierz and enrolled in the graduate school of canon law at the Catholic University of Lublin. After a month of vacation in Gdynia, I began my graduate studies in September 1956. About a month later, a bloody revolution erupted against Russian Communism in Hungary. Poland and East Germany expressed a degree of sympathy and solidarity with the Hungarians and did everything possible to help them. In Poland, university students and workers took to the streets, destroying many symbols of Russian Communism and demanding that both Cardinal Stefan Wyszynski and Wladyslaw Gomulka be freed from prison. The Communist government of Poland gave in to the demands of the masses and restored freedom to these two leaders and to many others. The Russian advisors to various governmental agencies packed and left for the Soviet Union. The persecution of the church stopped and the teaching of religion was restored in the public schools.

During this time, a very talented priest who taught religion in the Teachers' College in Radom ran into some trouble with the administration of the college and could no longer work there. Bishop Jan Kanty Lorek asked me to take the priest's place at the college. I had no choice and moved from Lublin to Radom. I was assigned to live at St. John the Baptist's rectory, where ten other priests lived. In my free time, I was to help in the parish, which at that time had thirty thousand members. It was a mega parish.

Three days a week I taught classes in the Teachers' College, three days I commuted by train to the university, and on Sundays I helped in the church. I was very busy, but my work was very challenging and very pleasant. Soon I discovered that my grade school principal in Sulislawice, Jan Pater, was now a headmaster of a technical school in Radom. He and his family provided me with very fine fellowship. The students in the college were very receptive to religious instruction and most pleasant to be with. I could not have asked for a better assignment.

## Chapter XI

My classes always began at 8:00 a.m. I walked from the rectory to the campus about three blocks away. In one of the blocks there was a large city hospital surrounded by an iron fence. One day, as I entered the faculty lounge before 8:00 a.m., its atmosphere appeared to be very gloomy. The faculty members were discussing something very serious. One of them asked me, "Did you hear the latest news?"

"What news?" I asked in return.

"The news about the patient in our hospital who was placed in the morgue before he expired," she informed me. Now I understood why everybody in the faculty lounge was so serious. Soon I learned that, through negligence, a seriously ill patient was taken to the morgue before he actually died. The patient's brother, who came to visit him was informed about the death and was taken to the morgue to see the body. During the viewing, the supposedly dead patient opened his eyes and looked into the face of his brother. The visiting brother was frightened beyond description and began to shout for help. Help arrived and the supposedly deceased man was taken back to his hospital room. The news of this tragic event began to spread all over the city like wildfire. The people were critical of the Communist way of operating the hospital.

The following day, a group of investigators from the Ministry of Health in Warsaw arrived at the hospital to conduct very embarrassing inquiries. They discovered that the hospital was guilty of serious negligence. During the inquiries, the patient's health improved considerably. Shortly thereafter, he was discharged from the hospital to live a meaningful life.

Our visit to Radom made me think about the priest who was the pastor of St. John the Baptist's Church, the mega parish. I do not remember meeting him before I came to the parish, although I knew a number of negative things about him from fellow priests in the diocese of Sandomierz. He belonged to a small group of priests who collaborated with the Communist government of Poland. The government called such priests "Patriot Priests".

These priests agreed with the Communist government that the Catholic Church of Poland should sever its ties with the Vatican and become an independent church. They were very reluctant to take orders from their bishops but accepted the orders of the atheistic directors of Religious Affairs, who, on the district level, represented the central government in Warsaw. These directors were appointed by the government not to improve the relationship between the state and the church but to hinder the activities of the church in every possible way. They had the power of *veto* over episcopal appointments to ecclesiastical offices, such as pastorates. In many instances, they used their power of *veto* so that numerous parishes were vacant for extended periods of time, to their detriment. In such cases, the directors promoted their own candidates from among the "Patriot Priests". If a bishop refused to grant the ecclesiastical jurisdiction to such a priest, a director of Religious Affairs had in his repertoire many ways of "persuading" him. So in many instances, to avoid a great evil, a bishop was forced to grant the jurisdiction to such a priest.

I always suspected that the priest who was my pastor at St. John the Baptist's Church had some misunderstandings with Bishop Jan Kanty Lorek before he began collaborating with the Communist government. I was almost sure that he did not become a "Patriot Priest" for theological or philosophical reasons. I never met a Catholic priest who was a Communist. The priesthood and Communism are incompatible. I did not condemn him; I felt sorry for him that he had chosen such a way of priestly life and ministry.

I visited him in his residence only one time; at the beginning of my ministry at St. John the Baptist's Church. For obvious reasons, he lived a very secluded life. His assistants, who had been in the parish for a long time, took good care of the parish. The pastor was more or less a figurehead. During my visit to his residence, he treated my very kindly and fraternally and wished me a successful ministry in the parish. After the visit, I had a very fine impression of him. If I am not mistaken, I never ran into him in the church or outside the church. He must have celebrated his Sunday and daily Masses at totally different times than I did.

Sometime in the spring of 1957, the pastor opted for another parish and left. An elderly priest took his place at St. John the Baptist's Church. He took the time to visit all of us priests attached to the church. He was forgetful and visited some of the priests twice without remembering it. When he came to my apartment, he was extremely surprised that I had a private telephone. Obviously, he was convinced that a telephone was an exclusive privilege of a pastor. When he asked me why I needed the telephone, I told him that as an instructor in the Teachers' College I needed to communicate with my fellow faculty and the students, and as a graduate student I had to be in touch with my professors. When I looked at his face, I knew that my arguments were less that convincing. The experience reminded me of an experience in the diocesan seminary in Sandomierz. As an administrator, I hired a plumber to install a small porcelain sink in the sacristy of the seminary church so the priests would have a chance to wash their hands before they went to the altar to celebrate Mass. One of the elderly priests on the faculty accused me of desecrating the holy place (sacristy) and noted that people who would see the sink would be inclined to think that priests come to the sacristy with unwashed hands.

By the time I finished recalling the experiences of my early priesthood in Radom, we had already left the suburbs of the city and were headed toward Kielce. We did not make any stops on the way.

Once we reached Kielce, we proceeded by the already well-known way to the residence of my friend. This time his daughter, a young physician, answered the door. After short introductions, she explained to us that her parents were staying for a few days in one of the villages near the city where they had a vegetable garden. She offered to go with us and show us the way to the village. We gladly accepted her offer and soon were on the way.

The village was about fifteen miles from the city of Kielce so it didn't take us long to reach it. It was a typical Polish village; houses on both sides of the street, with flower gardens in front of them and large orchards and vegetable gardens behind them.

My friend and his wife were pleasantly surprised to see us. We greeted each other warmly. My friend and I studied each other with curiosity. Thirty-three years had brought about some physical changes. I am sure we would not have recognized each other if we had met on the street. He is about five years older than I and had a very rough life under Communism in Poland. Nevertheless, he has preserved himself in a very good shape, both physically and mentally. At the end of World War II, he found himself in southern Germany. From there, he migrated to

Italy and then to England. After spending a short time in England, he returned to Poland with hopes of taking part in the rebuilding of the country. Unfortunately, his hopes were extinguished by the iron fist of Communism, which considered him a political enemy. As such, he was discriminated against in every phase of life. This discrimination caused him a great deal of suffering and bitterness. He wrote and attempted to publish a monograph on the World War II activities of our guerrilla unit, but the Communist censorship did not allow him. At the present time, he and his wife are retired and spend their summers in the country. Both of them love gardening and grow plenty of vegetables. They have converted part of a barn into a rustic and spacious dwelling.

During the meal, we recalled many of our mutual friends with whom we shared our lives and many events which became a part of us. As we conversed, I translated the most essential parts of our conversation for the benefit of my wife and our sons. I also translated questions and remarks of my family. The time flew fast in pleasant conversation. It was getting dark and we had to take my friend's daughter back to Kielce, so we said goodbye and left the dear and hospitable couple with hopes of visiting them again in the future. Before we left, my friend gave me a copy of the manuscript of his monograph and asked me to read it critically and return it to him with my comments.

After taking the young physician back to Kielce, we drove to our hotel in Polaniec. We were in the hotel at 11:30 p.m. We had a very long day and needed a well-deserved rest.

# Chapter XII

On Saturday, June 30, we stayed in Polaniec and rested. Since the stores close on Saturdays at 2:00 p.m., my wife went shopping in the morning and bought some food for the weekend. I got up early in the morning to read my friend's manuscript. It absorbed me totally. I couldn't do anything else but read it. Reading the manuscript brought back to my memory many persons and events that influenced my whole life.

In the afternoon, my wife and our sons went swimming while I continued reading the manuscript. We had dinner in the hotel. After dinner, our son Marian was invited by a group of teenagers to a disco dance. Of course he accepted the invitation and enjoyed the dance.

We began Sunday, July 1, with an early Holy Eucharist. After breakfast, we spent some time in the hotel and then drove to the cemetery in Osiek to visit my mother's grave. At the same time, we visited the graves of my godmother, Jozefa Kasprzycka, and her daughter, Henryka.

From Osiek, we went to Sulislawice to visit the graves of my father, grandparents, and other relatives. We also visited the parish church and prayed for a while. Then we drove to Gieraszowice to visit my sister Danuta and her family. We had dinner with them and spent a very pleasant evening.

On Monday, July 2, we drove to the city of Sandomierz, where we spent most of the day studying the history of my ancestors in the city's archives. The city archives building was located on a side street which ran parallel to the main street of Sandomierz. It was a narrow street that was seldom used. It reminded me of an experience which I had with a group of Gypsies during my work in the seminary.

I encountered the Gypsies in the city's commons, where about 150 of them pitched their tents and stayed for a couple of weeks. From my early youth, the Gypsies as an ethnic had interested and fascinated me. When I learned about their camp in the commons, I went to visit with them. Since I had read a couple of books about their origins, ethos, and language, and had picked up some expressions, I had no trouble attracting the Gypsy children. They eagerly came to me and helped me learn new Gypsy words and sayings. It was a delightful experience for me.

This experience led me to the idea of teaching catechism to these children. After consulting with some of the parents, I began daily instruction. After my work hours, day after day, I walked to the camp to teach the children for about one hour. As a rule, Gypsies accept the religion of the country in which they live their nomadic life. In Poland, they claim to be Roman Catholic; in Greece, Greek Orthodox. The Gypsy children were somewhat exposed to Christianity and received my informal classes very well.

After about a week of catechism classes, I invited the children and their parents to the seminary church for a Mass which I wanted to offer for all of them. They accepted my invitation with great joy. On the appointed day, I went to the camp at about 9:00 a.m. and led a group of about thirty-five children and adults to the church for the ten o'clock Mass. I knew that some people, and even some priests, might be surprised to see me with a band of Gypsies, so instead of taking the main street through the city, I took the side and narrow streets to avoid publicity. Nevertheless, some women who worked in their gardens noticed us and shouted to one another, "Look! A priest with the Gypsies! Isn't he ashamed to walk with them?" I could not believe my ears. Did not Christ associate with the poor, the needy, and the sinners? Didn't He say that those who are well do not need a physician, but those who are ill do? I realized that Gypsies in general did not have the best reputation in society, but they needed God and His teachings just like others.

I took the Gypsies to the seminary church (St. Michael's Church) and celebrated Mass for them. The children and their parents prayed with me and behaved in the church in the most proper way. It appeared to me that I was the first priest who had celebrated Mass in this historic church with a group of Gypsies. Since many of their relatives perished in the Nazi death camps, at the end of Mass we had special prayers for the repose of their relatives' souls. After the Mass was over, the Gypsies expressed warm gratitude to me. Their expression of gratitude was not only warm, but very authentic. I felt so good about my ministry to them. I wished I could have done more. The moments of my ministry to this group of Gypsies, even though very limited and sketchy, remained in my memory for such a long time, and as soon as we walked to the archives building located on the side and narrow street, I recollected those precious moments of my youthful ministry.

We had lunch in a popular restaurant below the castle of Sandomierz and visited the old part of the city. Late in the afternoon, we drove to Jeziory to spend the evening with my brother Robert and his family.

The following day, Tuesday, July 3, we started our journey to the city of Szczekociny, where my sister Henryka lives. The weather was beautiful and driving was very pleasant. We were driving west. On the way, we stopped for about one hour in the very old town of Chenciny, where we visited a museum and the ruins of a very impressive castle which was built during the reign of Casimir the Great (1333-1370).

After we left Chenciny, we kept driving through very picturesque country toward Szczekociny. Soon we made another stop at a beautiful manor whcih was well-preserved and had been converted into a museum containing memorabilia of Mikolaj (Michael) Rej, (1505-1569), a famous Polish poet who lived and wrote during the period of time when literature in Poland was making the transition from the Latin language to Polish. He was proud to write in Polish and encouraged others to do so.

During the tour, we admired the architecture of the manor and shared our feelings with a curator. She obviously detected in us a love for antiquity and suggested that we visit another manor which had been abandoned by the latest residents and was located not far from the highway on which we traveled.

After completing our tour or the well-preserved manor, we drove to see the abandoned one. When we arrived there, we couldn't see the manor house at first because it was hidden in a large park. Soon we found the driveway and parked in front of the main entrance of a beautifully constructed Renaissance manor which was in a deplorable condition. Most of the windows on the first floor were boarded. The windows on the second floor were broken. The front door was boarded and the side door was torn out. One of the chimneys had collapsed on a section of the roof, which had caused the roof to cave in. As we stood in front of the manor house deploring its condition, a group of children came to see us. I engaged them in conversation and learned from them that they lived in a long house in which there were many apartments for farm workers. Two of the children told me that their father was the manager of the farm. Soon we met their father and obtained his permission to visit the manor house.

When we walked into the house, we could not believe our eyes. It was in a terrible state. Plaster was coming off the ceilings and walls on account of rain water falling through the damaged roof. Some floors were stripped of boards, and all sorts of garbage was everywhere. This is what Communism did to the beautiful manor house in Rzeszowek.

After visiting the manor house, we walked in the park full of unusual and beautiful grown trees. Then we went to the manager's office to say goodbye to him and thank him for letting us visit the manor. He explained to us that when the Communist government assumed power in Poland toward the end of World War II, Piotr Borkowski and his wife were the owners of the Rzeszowek manor house and an extensive acreage of land which surrounded it. As in the case of other manors and lands in the country, the Communist authorities nationalized the Borkowski property and expelled the owners from their home. The Borkowskis found shelter in Cracow, where they lived until their death.

The manager told us that since the manor house deteriorated very rapidly, the local government was eager to sell the property for a nominal price on the condition that the new owner would restore the manor house and preserve it. When I asked the manager about the rightful owners of the property, he replied that the Borkowskis had died without an heir and after the collapse of the Communist government no one came to claim the estate. After saying all these things, he encouraged us to buy the manor house, the park, and some acreage. We were excited about the prospect of purchasing the property but at the same time we realized that restoration of the manor house would be next to impossible because of the shortage of building materials in Poland.

From the manor of Rzeszowek, we continued our journey to my sister's home in Szczekociny. It didn't take us long to reach the city. We found her home without any trouble. We parked our car in front of the house and knocked on the door. She answered the door and recognized us immediately. It was a joy to see her and her husband, Edward Baran, after thirty-three years. Their son was not at home; he was taking an entrance examination at the University of Wroclaw. My sister and her husband regretted that he was not home to meet us and spend some time with us. We also regretted not being able to meet him.

During the meal, my sister and I recollected many events from our childhood and teenage years. I had a chance to get acquainted with my brother-in-law, whom I had never met in person. When I left Poland in 1957, my sister was married to her first husband, Zygmunt Grzelka, a school principal who died at an early age. A few years after his death, my sister married Edward, who was a widower.

It must have been about 4:00 p.m. when we left the hospitable home of Henryka and Ed and began our journey toward Czestochowa. We kept driving west.

At about 7:00 p.m., we stopped at a very unusual hotel on the edge of a large forest. The hotel was built on a gentle slope of a hill. Below it there was a beautiful lake. It was a wonderful place to relax and spend vacation.

After checking in and carrying our suitcases to our rooms, we took a walk on the spacious grounds of the resort. Soon our sons went swimming in the lake and made friends with a group of boys who were boating and swimming there. My wife and I watched the young people play in the water.

When our sons came out of the lake and changed, all of us drove around to see the area. We came across a beautiful palace which had belonged to a very wealthy family. The Communist authorities converted it into a school of agriculture. The surroundings of the palace included flower gardens, an orchard, a lake, and a very large park. We walked around and admired the beauty of the architecture and the landscape. It was already dark when we returned to our hotel. We had had a long and eventful day.

## Chapter XIII

On Wednesday, July 4, we were on our feet early in the morning and resumed our journey to Czestochowa. After driving for about three hours, we came to the city of Olsztyn. The ruins of the ancient castle caught our interest. We all decided to see the castle before breakfast. We climbed a very high hill on which the castle was built. Again, it was a defensive castle constructed during the reign of King Casimir the Great. The castle begged to be restored to its previous glory.

After visiting the castle and taking many pictures of our sons and the ruins, we found a restaurant in Olsztyn where we could have breakfast. The restaurant was very nice and clean. For a while, we were the only ones in one of the rooms. As soon as we began to eat our breakfast, however, an elderly man entered the room and took a table next to ours. When he heard us speak English, he attempted to communicate with us in his limited German. When I explained to him that I spoke Polish, he was very happy and began to speak to me continuously without interruption. After a while, I tried to interrupt the conversation in order to finish my breakfast and to converse with my family, but he would not let me. He talked like a machine gun. I found myself in a very embarrassing situation. My family ate in silence and I could not finish my food. Then he called a waitress and ordered whiskey for himself and for all of us. I explained to him that we do not drink alcohol when we travel by car. He accepted my explanation and told me that I was excused as a driver but that my wife and our sons should take a drink. I further explained to him that it is not customary for us to drink anything alcoholic in the morning. He would not listen to my explanation and kept insisting that my wife and our sons should partake of the drinks which the waitress, in the meantime, had brought to his table. When his insistence became increasingly forceful, we paid for our breakfast and left the restaurant. We could not think of a better way of extricating ourselves from the embarrassing situation.

After leaving the restaurant, we went to a bookstore to see the newest publications and buy a few books. Then we continued our journey.

We were in the suburbs of the city of Czestochowa before lunch. The traffic was rather heavy. Even though I had visited the city a couple of times before, I did not know which street led to the National Shrine of Our Lady of Czestochowa. Downtown, I asked for directions, and soon we were driving toward Jasna Gora (Bright Mountain), on the top of which the shrine and the monastery were built in medieval times. It was raining and the visibility was so poor that we could hardly see the tower of the shrine which dominates the whole area.

Soon we came very close to the walls of the shrine and found a parking lot. From the parking lot we walked about one-half mile to the main gate in the walls. As we entered the grounds of the sacred shrine, we were full of spiritual ardor. We caught the spirit of the pilgrims who came there before us. We went directly to the shrine. As we entered it, the shrine was packed with pilgrims. The priest at the altar of Our Lady of Czestochowa was chanting the concluding prayers of High Mass. Soon the miraculous image of Our Lady was veiled. I felt disappointed because I wanted so much for my family to see the famous image of Our Lady of Czestochowa and offer prayers at the altar of God with the unveiled sacred picture. My disappointment soon changed to great joy as a group of Japanese pilgrims entered the chapel of Our Lady and their priests approached the altar to lead the people in celebration of Mass.

As the Japanese pilgrims sang an opening song, the miraculous image was unveiled. We thanked God for His grace. The Japanese songs and chanting of prayers sounded very unusual to our ears but at the same time accentuated the universality of Christianity which transcends race, color of skin, language, culture, and continents.

During the Mass, I thanked God for the privilege of visiting the shrine for the third time. I prayed for my wife and our sons, for the parishioners of St. Paul's Church, and for all relatives and friends. I prayed also for the souls of those dear ones who had died. As I looked into the sacred image of Our Lady, I saw in her face love and compassion. At the same time, I felt that her loving eyes penetrated my whole being. I had the same experience when on May 28, 1952, I celebrated my first Mass at the altar of God in the chapel of Our Lady of Czestochowa. Then I was one of twenty-one in my ordination class who came to the shrine of Our Lady of Czestochowa to prayerfully begin our priestly ministry.

According to an old legend, the sacred image of Our Lady of Czestochowa was painted by St. Luke on the table which the Blessed Virgin Mary used when she lived in Ephesus after the death of her son, Jesus Christ. From Ephesus, the sacred image was brought to the church built by the Pauline Fathers, where it became known as a miraculous image because many persons experienced healing when they prayed to God at the chapel of Our Lady.

The shrine of Our Lady of Czestochowa acquired great fame and prominence during the Swedish wars in Poland. In 1655, Swedish King Charles X (known also as Charles Gustavus) and his army invaded Poland and managed to occupy the entire country with the exception of Jasna Gora. A handful of soldiers and monks, under the leadership of Father Kordecki, prior of the monastery, withstood a brutal Swedish siege for forty days. The Swedish army was forced to withdraw. This ignited a spontaneous and heroic resistance of the Polish people against the army of the invader. In a short time, the Swedish army suffered a decisive defeat and left Poland. The people of Poland had no doubt that this chain of events was a great miracle wrought by God through the intercession of Our Lady. Shortly thereafter, Polish King John Casimir proclaimed the Mother of Christ as the Queen of Poland. Soon the church on Jasna Gora which enshrined the miraculous image of Our Lady of Czestochowa became a national shrine. As such, it became the spiritual heart of the nation.

During the partitions of Poland by Russia, Prussia, and Austria, the National Shrine of Our Lady of Czestochowa became a unifying factor for all Poles inhabiting various parts of Poland. During subsequent uprisings of the Polish people against the occupying powers, the people and their leaders sought spiritual strength through the instumentality of the shrine and the intercession of Our Lady of Czestochowa. During the crucial events of World War I, from which Poland emerged a unified and free nation, the shrine of Our Lady played a very important role. During the Nazi invasion of Poland in 1939 and the occupation that followed, the National Shrine of Our Lady of Czestochowa was the source of hope and spiritual power of the Polish people. When the Soviet brand of Communism forced itself on Poland after World War II, the pilgrimages of workers, farmers, teachers, lawyers, physicians, university professors, high school youth, university students, etc., to the national shrine brought about a rejuvenation of Christianity and its immense spiritual and moral energies: the energies with which materialistic and godless communism was unable to cope. In present times, when the reconstruction of democratic institutions is taking place in the country, the National Shrine of Our Lady of Czestochowa exercises a great spiritual influence on the Polish people. At the same time, the presence of the Japenese Christians in the chapel of Our Lady with whom we participated in the Holy Eucharist gives evidence that the shrine has also a religious influence on nations outside Poland.

When the Japanese Holy Eucharist ended and before we went to visit other parts of the shrine, I explained to my family that shortly after the Nazi invasion of Poland in 1939, the agents of Hitler's government in Germany showed a great interest in ancient and sacred art in the country. In some instances, they seized various pieces of art and transferred them to Germany. When the prior of the Pauline Monastery at Jasna Gora received an official letter from Berlin telling him that a group of German art experts was about to visit the national shrine and examine various objects of art there, he and his monks began to fear that the Nazis might seize the sacred image of Our Lady of Czestochowa. In order to prevent such a possibility, one of the monks, who was an excellent painter, made an identical reproduction of the ancient image of Our Lady of Czestochowa. He used an old board on which to paint the sacred picture. As soon as the paint had dried somewhat, the original was removed from the altar in utmost secrecy and hidden in a safe place. The replica was then placed above the altar.

When the Nazi art experts arrived at Jasna Gora, they insisted on examining the picture of Our Lady of Czestochowa. The monks were full of fear. The prior and the monk who had painted the replica feared for their lives. During the examination of the sacred image, the painter himself assisted the art experts and gave them an account of the legendary origin of the sacred painting. The experts appeared to be impressed and declared very seriously that the picture gave all indications of having been painted in the Middle East at the outset of the Christian era. The monk who had painted the very picture which the Nazi experts examined in his presence and with his help could not laugh at the expertise of the Nazis because fear froze his laughter. After the experts left Jasna Gora, the monk-painter and the prior were convinced that either the Nazi experts were not experts at all or they were experts whose vision was miraculously distorted like the vision of those Swedish artillerymen who could not aim well at the shrine because they suffered from optical illusions.

As we stood in the chapel of Our Lady looking at the miraculous image, one of our sons noticed that on the face of Our Lady's image there were two straight lines like cuts. He wanted to know the origin of these marks. I explained that according to old tradition, these marks were made by a fanatical Bohemian soldier who, as a follower of an early religious reformer, disapproved the veneration of Our Lady. He was part of a large Bohemian force which invaded the southwestern part of Poland, including Czestochowa. When the invaders entered the shrine unexpectedly, to desecrate it, one of the religious fanatics went to the chapel of Our Lady, drew his sword, and cut twice the face of the image of the Mother of Jesus Christ. Since that time (most probably the first part of the fifteenth century), the marks of the sword have remained on the face of Our Lady of Czestochowa. They can be seen on all photographs of the sacred picture.

Before we left the National Shrine of Our Lady of Czestochowa, we knelt down and prayed for our safe journey to my brother Eugene's home in the northwestern part of Poland. He was the last brother we were to visit before returning to Germany.

Soon we were on the way to the city of Wroclaw. We were driving west. From Wroclaw, we intended to proceed north. After we drove for a while, we needed rest and looked for a hotel. For this purpose, we took an exit to a small town. There was no hotel in the traditional sense of the word; however, there was a workers' hotel which had vacancies. The clerk at the desk told us that the hotel had no hot water. The rooms were neat and spacious. The price for overnight accommodation was fabulously low--about $1.75 per room with two beds. We were tempted to take the rooms, but we needed a hot bath. So we decided to continue our journey to the next town along the highway in hopes of finding a traditional hotel. The next town was the city of Opole. In the suburbs of Opole, we found another workers' hotel, but we decided to drive downtown to see whether we could find something better. Indeed, we found the Kasztelanski Hotel. For two large rooms, we paid $45.00. The hotel's restaurant was closed for repairs.

After taking a needed bath, we had dinner in our hotel room. Then we went to see the historic downtown area of Opole. We were impressed by the beauty of architecture and the antiquity of the churches and public buildings. It was getting dark when we returned to our hotel to rest well before the final leg of our journey to my brother's home in Debno Lubuskie.

# Chapter XIV

The early part of Thursday, July 5, we spent in Opole. Since the restaurant in our hotel was closed, my wife and I went to the railroad station restaurant for breakfast. We enjoyed the fresh and tasty food served there. From the restaurant, we returned to our hotel. On our way back, we bought some food and milk for our sons, who still rested in the hotel. While our sons were having their breakfast, I went to a hotel barbershop to have my hair cut and then I went to a bank near the hotel to exchange some of our currency.

At about 9:00 a.m., we were on our way toward Wroclaw. The highway was excellent. After we reached the suburbs of the city of Wroclaw, we kept going toward Lubin and Zielona Gora. We had lunch in a very modern restaurant near the city of Zielona Gora. During lunch, we noticed through the window that three or four boys about twelve years old had approached our car and were beginning to do something to it. I was afraid they might want to take the windshield wipers so I knocked on the window to let them know we were watching them and then went to the car to see what was going on. There I discovered that the boys wanted to "dry clean" our car for a certain fee. Since the car had some dirt on it, I was afraid the "dry cleaning" might be harmful to its paint, so I asked the boys to forget about the cleaning job.

After lunch, we kept driving north toward the city of Gorzow Wielkopolski. Soon we took some secondary highways and came close to my brother's hometown, Debno Lubuskie. In a nice town near Debno Lubuskie, we found a very reasonable and hospitable hotel and took two rooms. Since we were near the German border, we had to give our passports to the hotel clerk. Having taken our suitcases to our rooms, we drove to Debno Lubuskie to visit my brother and his family. A man on a motorcycle who was about to go fishing gave us directions to my brother's residence. In a while, we were parking our car in front of my brother's modern house. He lives on a corner lot of a quiet residential section of town. My sister-in-law answered the door and invited us into the house. Since my brother married after I left for the United States, I did not personally know her. She knew right away who we were, though, and called her husband. He came to the hallway to greet us in a warm, traditionally Polish greeting. Soon we were in the living room talking about ourselves and our families--another joyful family reunion after thirty-three years.

Before my sister-in-law asked us to come to the dining room for dinner, she called her mother and invited her to have dinner with us. As our conversations developed, the atmosphere of my brother's home became increasingly warmer and more and more loving.

While speaking about himself, my brother told me about his academic and sports successes in the school of agriculture. Then he told me about his first job as a supervisor of a couple of farming cooperatives. His hard work and honesty set him on a collision course with the Communist apparatchiks who wanted him to work in such a way as to cover up their unpardonable ignorance and mistakes. When he refused, he was interrogated and brutally tortured by agents of the secret security police. In spite of torture and threats of imprisonment, Eugene did not compromise his principles. Later on, the Communist apparatchiks left him alone because they had to recognize his excellent moral and intellectual qualities. After the disintegration of the Communist government in the country, my brother could have taken legal action against the agents of the secret police who tortured him, but he is not a vengeful person.

Even though Eugene is too young to retire, he spoke to me about his retirement that was precipitated by a back injury caused by a bicycle accident. Being in an excellent physical shape all his life, he cannot reconcile himself to his present disability. Tears came to his eyes when he talked to me about this. Fortunately, his new house was built before the accident.

When I asked my brother about his assessment of the present political situation in Poland, he made a very shocking statement. He said, "Marian, let me be honest with you and say what I feel. Since the end of World War II until the most recent times, we lived under the red Communism; and after the collapse of the Communist government in Poland, we began to live under the black Communism." When I asked him what he meant by "the black Communism", my brother replied, "The clergy." He continued, "Nothing happens now in Poland without the blessing of the clergy. The bishops interfere in all the affairs of the state. Why don't they let laypeople take care of the business of the state and limit themselves to the affairs of the Church? Please do not misunderstand me. I am a believer and a practicing Catholic. I attend Mass every Sunday."

I could not believe my ears when I heard what he said. During the weeks of our visit in Poland, no one had told me anything like this.

During further conversation, I became convinced that Eugene's honest opinion about clerical interference into the affairs of the state was shared by mature and educated laity in Poland. If the church-state relationship does not move toward a healthy separation, there will be a rise of anticlericalism. History will repeat itself and the pre-World War II anticlericalism will return to Poland with all its negative consequences.

My sister-in-law served a fantastic dinner which we enjoyed very much. During dinner, we spoke mostly about various members of our family and relatives. We learned that Eugene and his wife have two grownup children: Marius and Beata. They live away from home.

After the meal, my brother suggested that we bring in our suitcases and stay with them overnight. He was disappointed to hear that we had left our suitcases at the hotel.

We left my brother's hospitable home at about 9:30 p.m. and drove to our hotel for our last night in Poland.

## Chapter XV

On Friday, July 6, we were up at 6:00 a.m., had breakfast in the hotel's restaurant, and began to drive to Berlin at 7:00 a.m. On the Polish-German border, we went through a checkpoint near the German city of Frankfurt on the Oder River. The highway from Frankfurt to Berlin was excellent and straight. When we reached the vicinity of Berlin, we took the beltway and entered that part of the city which before the unification was known as East Berlin. It must have been about 9:30 a.m. We parked our car in East Berlin and walked about three-hundred feet to the infamous Berlin Wall. An opening in the wall was already made for street traffic. The wall was higher than I had imagined but not as thick as I had thought. It was built of large sections of concrete.

At the wall, we met a nice German family from whom we borrowed masonry tools to cut some pieces of the wall as mementos for our sons. The concrete wall was very hard and we had considerable trouble cutting a few fragments from it. On the Communist side of the wall there was a guardhouse which somebody had hurriedly converted into a service station.

From the wall, we walked to the West Germany section of Berlin. It was almost noontime and we were hungry and thirsty so we went to a small restaurant to have lunch. There we discovered that our East German currency was already worthless. The time for exchanging it had already passed when we were in Poland. Fortunately, we had enough West German marks to pay for our sons' lunch. My wife and I waited for our lunch until we returned to our car, in which we had plenty of food. Since there was some official holiday in Germany, the banks were closed. There was no way of exchanging our U.S. currency.

After wandering in West Berlin for a couple of hours, we began our trip to Nuremberg. We took again the Berlin beltway, drove by Postsdam, and headed toward the south of Germany.

The highway was very good and the weather was warm. In the late afternoon, we came close to Leipzig and were tempted to stay in this famous city for the night; however, my wife encouraged me to drive directly to Nuremberg, so we kept driving. Soon we crossed the highway which in the early part of our journey we took from Eisenach to Dresden and then to Poland. It was already dark when we drove by the city of Bayreuth, where the German musical genius and philosopher Richard Wagner established his well-known musical center in which he hoped the Greek tragedy would be resurrected.

We reached the suburbs of the city of Nuremberg at about 11:30 p.m. and found an excellent hotel, but it was extremely expensive so we decided to drive to the old part of the city, which our son Joseph and I knew well. We hoped to find accommodations in the Pension Adler in which we stayed two years ago. As we were trying to reach the historic part of the city, the darkness of the night and the lights made certain sections of the city look different and hard to find. Finally we found a well-known street and reached the area of the city we were looking for. Now parking our car became a problem. After driving from one street to another, we found a space to park our car. My wife and our son Marian stayed in the car while Joseph and I went to search for hotel rooms. The Pension Adler had no vacancy, so we went to other places and eventually located a decent and reasonable hotel. It was about 1:00 a.m. When we checked into the hotel, we were physically and emotionally exhausted. After taking showers, we were in bed by 2:00 a.m. and rested during the remainder of the night.

On Saturday, July 7, we slept until 9:00 a.m. and had a late breakfast. After the continental breakfast, we went to the downtown bank to exchange our currency. We had no trouble exchanging the American currency, but when we attempted again to exchange our East German currency, we were told that it had lost its value. It was only a few days after the unification of the two Germanys and already East German marks were not worth the paper on which they were printed. Fortunately, we had only a small amount of East German money.

From the bank, we went to the Pension Adler and reserved two rooms until July 13. Our son Joseph and I had stayed there before and liked it more than the hotel in which we stayed the night before. After shopping for a while in the section of the old city, we returned to the hotel, packed our suitcases, and moved to the Pension Adler. Soon we found a parking garage for our car within a short distance from the pension. Now we were free to relax and visit the city. Our son Joseph and I were eager to show it to the other half of our family. As we walked the streets of the ancient city, we stopped from time to time to listen to the street musicians who played various instruments for the benefit of passersby. Among the street musicians we found two groups of Inca Indians from South America who came to Germany to make some money. They played some unusual instruments. The people liked them very much. We did, too, and gave them ten marks.

During our visit to the old city, we visited St. Mary's and St. Laurence churches and admired the ancient art of Durer and Veit Stoss. We also went to see antique shops and art galleries. We walked and walked until we became tired and hungry. Then we had lunch--a good German lunch. In the afternoon, our sons decided to go to the city on their own so they could see what interested them. They did not want to eat dinner with us at a German restaurant but instead wanted to go to the McDonald's restaurant which was near our pension. My wife and I had our dinner in one of the restaurants in the old city. In the evening, we returned to our pension to enjoy its comforts.

On Sunday, July 8, we were up at 9:00 a.m. During breakfast in the pension, we met two American students from Georgetown University in Washington, D.C., and engaged in a conversation with them. We spoke about religion in Europe and America and about the political scene in Europe.

After breakfast, we got ready to attend St. Clara's Church, which was almost next door to the pension. The Mass was scheduled for 11:15 a.m. The Jesuit Order is now in charge of the church, which was built before the Reformation. During the Reformation, it was taken over by the reformers and held by them until the most recent times. Since the secularization of the reformed (Lutheran) churches is progressing very rapidly, St. Clara'a Church lost its parishioners and was returned to the Roman Catholics. The Jesuits extended their jurisdiction over the old church and filled it with enthusiastic crowds of worshippers. St. Clara's Church is not an exception in Nuremberg. Other churches in the city went through a similar process.

The Mass which we attended at 11:15 a.m. was celebrated in Spanish. The church was packed with people. There was no choir, but the congregation sang joyfully and enthusiastically. Men, women, teenagers,and children sang in unison. A young lady directed the congregation in singing. We did our best to follow the others in singing. Our spirits were uplifted and put in the spirit of worship. It was wonderful to be in the midst of the enthusiastic worshipping community.

Following the Mass, we intended to have lunch in an Italian restaurant near the marketplace. Our sons, however, preferred to eat at McDonald's instead. So our sons went to McDonald's and my wife and I walked to the Italian restaurant. The restaurant was on the second floor. The hostess seated us at a table where an elderly couple sat. The lady and the gentleman welcomed us to the table and introduced themselves to us. They were Mr. and Mrs. Heinz Tieman--a very pleasant and friendly couple. During lunch, Mr. Tieman told us that he was retired from a large paper company and was enjoying his retirement. He was happy about the West German economic stability and expressed a hope that this stability would continue after the unification. Mrs. Tieman talked to us about her family, especially about her mother, who was anti-Nazi and died in Dachau. She also told us that many Turks who came to Germany during the postwar economic boom act like the Nazis and murder innocent people on the streets of German cities. When talking about the crimes committed by some of the Turkish immigrants, she was in tears because one of her friends, a pregnant young woman, was stabbed to death by one of them. She felt that the biggest problem which West Germany was facing now was not an economic burden resulting from the unification, but the Turkish immigrants.

As we ate our dinner and talked, the atmosphere at the table became warmer and warmer. My wife and I were very happy that the hostess had seated us at the same table with this lovely German couple. Toward the end of our dinner, Mr. Tieman ordered a fine Italian liquor for all of us. My wife and I were grateful to him and appreciated his kindness. It was a beautiful and friendly gesture on his part. If I am not mistaken, it took us about two hours to eat our dinner. The time went very fast because of such agreeable company.

After we expressed our gratitude to the German couple for their wonderful company and the drinks, we returned to our pension and asked our sons to go with us to the famous museum of Nuremberg. They were glad to go. Joseph and I had been in the museum of Nuremberg on the previous occasion. After one hour of visiting various sections of the museum, we were very tired and decided to return to our quarters. At the pension, I read and translated for the benefit of my wife a book of memoirs written by Rudolf Höss, who was in charge of the Auschwitz death camp.

Our restful evening was interrupted by a noisy celebration on the street. Our sons went to the main street to see what was happening. After a while, Joseph returned and reported that the young people of Nuremberg were celebrating the victory of the German soccer team in one of the South American countries. Thousands of young people took to the streets, dancing and shouting "Deutschland, Deutschland, Deutschland--Victory, Victory, Victory". Our younger son, Marian, joined the young people in their celebration and did not return to the pension until 1:00 a.m. We worried about his safety and searched for him among the crowds of young people. He told us later that he was riding in a car with German teenagers, shouting "Deutschland, Deutschland . . ."

On Monday, July 9, my wife, Joseph, and I went shopping. Marian had to stay in his room until 3:00 p.m. as punishment for not returning to the pension in time the night before. After our morning of shopping, we returned to the pension for lunch so our Marian would not be too lonely.

In the afternoon, I rested for an hour while my wife and Joseph went shopping again. We had dinner in the pension. Following dinner, my wife and I went to town for a long walk. Our sons also went to town on their own. In the evening, we packed our clothing in preparation for our trip to Frankfurt.

## Chapter XVI

On Tuesday, July 10, we were up early in the morning. Following breakfast in the pension, we went to say goodbye to Father Übelmesser, a Jesuit priest who helped our Joseph study the German language during our previous visit in Nuremberg. Father Übelmesser was happy to see us and offered a prayer for our safe journey to Frankfurt and to the States.

Soon we were on our way to the city of Frankfurt. The highway was excellent. We made only a couple of stops to get gasoline and to have our lunch. By about 4:00 p.m., we reached Frankfurt Airport. Since we did not know the city of Frankfurt, we decided to stay in the Hilton Hotel at the airport. The rates were high but the accommodations were excellent. We were fortunate to get the rooms at that time of the day. On the second floor of the hotel there was a passage to the airport. Our car was parked in the underground public parking near the hotel. We had our dinner in the hotel. After dinner, we went to explore the extensive shopping areas under the airport buildings. We were impressed by the great abundance in the stores and the excellent order at the airport.

On Wednesday, July 11, we had an early breakfast and then took our suitcases to the airport. While my wife and our sons were checking in our luggage at the U.S. Air counter, I went to return the car to the Avis Company. Having done this, I joined my family at the U.S. Air counter. Our luggage was already being checked in. I worried about the three metal gasoline containers which we bought in Poland and decided to take home with us to the U.S.A. The day before, I emptied the containers and aired them under the car in the parking garage. During the electronic checking of our luggage, the German attendants examined them and let them go. We were happy about it because the containers were far superior to American gasoline containers.

## Chapter XVI

Shortly after 10:30 a.m., we boarded a U.S. Air jet bound for Pittsburgh, Pennsylvania. We were relieved and happy to go home. Our jet took off at 11:00 a.m. and we were on our way to the United States. Excellent meals and company made our flight very pleasant. We landed in the Pittsburgh Airport at about 6:00 p.m. of the same day. While Joseph and I claimed our luggage, my wife and Marian went to get our car from the parking lot near the airport. Soon we were on our way home to enjoy its comforts and rest after a month of exciting experiences in Poland, West Germany, and East Germany. My going home to Poland after thirty-three years enriched me and my family both spiritually and psychologically. We thanked God for the precious opportunity.

# Part II
# World War II True Stories

## Chapter I

## The First Action of Our Flying Commando

The night was dark on Thursday, November 11, 1943. An autumn rain had been falling for several days. We were walking like ducks in a row behind Captain "Kaktus" (Tadeusz Strus), wading practically up to our ankles through drenched fields. No one except our leader knew where we were going. Along the way, we passed many villages which dotted the darkness of the night with dim light from their oil lamps. Here and there could be heard the barking of dogs.

After several hours of wearisome marching, our group, consisting at that time of twelve persons, reached the village of Kamien Plebanski, which was located in the general area of hilly country known as Pieprzowki. There we stopped to rest in two houses standing apart from the village. The captain assigned the hours of watch and ordered the rest of us to go to sleep as soon as possible. Tired and weary, we fell into a deep sleep on the straw spread out on the floor.

Following our morning awakening and a breakfast, the captain called in a few of us at a time for a conference. On the table in the captain's room were lying the plans of a rather large building and various notes. The captain, as usual at such times, immediately came to the point. We were to take control of a building which served as the quarters for approximately fifty Germans. Most of them were railroad police (*Bahnschutzpolizei*) and Air Force (*Luftwaffe*) men. The purpose of our action was to disarm the Germans and thus secure for us badly needed weapons. The captain, therefore, was acquainting each of us with the layout of the building and giving us our assignments. The time of this action was set for the evening. Despite the discomfort of the previous day, our faces beamed with joy and enthusiasm in anticipation of the coming action.

The rest of the day we spent cleaning our weapons and checking and rechecking their proper functioning. Finally, evening came. We hurriedly put on our long topcoats, hiding underneath them our pistols and hand grenades. One of our men who was assigned to operate a light machine gun found the task of hiding his weapon under his topcoat a little more difficult, but he finally succeeded in doing so.

It was dusky outside when we started on our way to Sandomierz. We had to be at our destination at 18 Mickiewicza Street at 7:00 p.m., when the majority of the Germans would be sitting down to supper in the large dining hall. We marched through fields, thereby avoiding Sandomierz to the south. On one of the side roads, we captured, accidentally, a policeman who happened to be in the German service. The unfortunate man kept justifying himself and pleading for forgiveness. He promised to cease all work with the German police. After searching him, we released him with the admonition not to mention to anyone that he had met us.

Coming into the section of the town bustling with activity and people, we split up into pairs in order not to attract the attention of the German police patrolling the streets. Thus mingling with passersby, we finally arrived at our destination. Before our eyes stood a large three-story building. A concrete sidewalk connected the city sidewalk to the building. At its main entrance there was a dim electric light. The door to the building was closed and a uniformed guard stood in front of it. On the western side of the building there was a side door also with a light above it but it was not guarded.

The action began when "Iskra" (Arkadiusz Swiercz), wearing a uniform of the German railroad police (*Bahnschutzpolizei*), appeared in front of the building, briskly walked toward the guard, and saluted him with "Heil Hitler." As soon as he passed the guard, he pulled out his pistol, put it to the guard's back, and softly said to him, *"Still! Hande hoch!"** Without uttering a word, the guard raised his hands and let

*Quiet! Hands up!

"Iskra" take his pistol. At that point in time, two of our machine gun men took their positions on the porch of the neighboring building and the rest of us, under the leadership of Captain "Kaktus", began to enter the building by the side door. As soon as we entered the building, all of us, mostly in pairs, went to our assigned positions.

Captain "Kaktus" led "Jach" (Wlodimierz Gruszczynski) and "Smigly" (Henryk Dudek) to the dining hall, where over thirty Germans, totally oblivious to what was happening around them, were sitting at the dinner tables. Only the captain's order *"Hande hoch!"* and the barrels of three pistols made them aware of their situation. A deathly silence fell. The Germans stood up in their places and raised their hands. Three German women who were in the dining hall were also asked to raise their hands. Both Captain "Kaktus" and "Jach", who spoke German, ordered the Germans to approach, with hands raised, the main wall in the dining room, face it, and put their palms against it. They obediently executed the order. This enabled our men to search each person individually and disarm them one by one. Before all the Germans were disarmed in the dining hall, "Iskra" brought in the guard that he had disarmed in front of the building. The captain ordered the guard to stand against the wall with the others. Then "Iskra" returned to keep guard in front of the building. During the disarming in the dining hall, the three women were disarmed as well. From one of the women, "Smigly" took a small pistol, with which he accidentally shot himself in the hand.

After the disarmament of the Germans in the dining hall was completed, Captain "Kaktus" and "Smigly" went to the second floor to help the others while "Jach" remained in the dining hall to guard the Germans. As "Jach" stood in the middle of the dining hall and watched the backs of the uniformed Germans, he became aware that one of the Germans, who was his size, wore a very well-cut uniform. He decided to trade his old and worn-out high school uniform for it. The German officer who wore the pretty uniform was not happy at all to trade clothes with "Jach", but "Jach's" order gave him no alternative. He undressed at the wall and threw the uniform toward "Jach". "Jach" also asked for the officer's boots. "Jach" then undressed and put on the uniform and the boots. Both of them were a perfect fit. After a short while, "Jach" forced the unlucky German to wear his wet clothes and muddy shoes. "Jach" realized then how poorly his high school suit looked on the new owner.

In the meantime, a number of us rushed to the second and third floors of the building. As we climbed the stairs between the first and the second floor, we noticed that there was a sort of extended stairway landing where the Germans placed their telephone switchboard. "Straceniec" (Jan Osemlak), who had previous experience with telephone switchboards, quickly disabled it.

When we reached the second floor, Captain "Kaktus", "Cap" (Marian Gaj) and a number of others burst into the rooms on the left side of the hallway and began to disarm the Germans. In one of the rooms which "Cap" entered, all the Germans raised their hands with the exception of one, who began to reach for his pistol. "Cap" shouted *"Hande hoch"* for a second time, and when the German did not raise his hands, "Cap" aimed at him and squeezed the trigger of his Stayer. Fortunately for the German, there was a misfire. Now realizing that "Cap" was not joking, the German raised his hands in a hurry. "Cap" reloaded and disarmed the Germans. In order to punish the German who reached for his gun, "Cap" ordered him to lie down on the hallway floor.

In another room, Captin "Kaktus" was disarming a group of Germans. One of them asked the captain to let him keep his World War I artillery Luger (long barrel), which was a memento given to him by his father. The captain was sympathetic but unbending. The German had to give up his beautiful and valuable pistol. In this situation, our captain could not afford sentimentality. He was a leader of a group of young men who fought for their own lives and for the life of the nation. When the German kept pleading for his pistol, the captain ordered him to prostrate himself on the floor in the hallway.

"Blyskawica" (Boleslaw Szelong) and I were assigned to disarm the German pilots who occupied the third floor. "Straceniec" was to join us a few moments later. In the meantime, the two of us rushed quietly to the third floor where the pilots from two adjoining rooms (dormitories) gathered together for a small celebration which appeared to be a birthday party. Most of them were sitting around a table full of food which appeared to have come from their families in Germany. The pilots were totally relaxed; their tunics and belts with pistols were hanging on chairs and a hallway tree. They were eating, drinking, and talking.

When "Blyskawica" and I entered the room, the pilots interrupted their conversation and, their faces full of surprise, turned toward us. We pointed our pistols at them and I said, half smiling, *"Guten Abend Herren"*.* Before they could respond, I ordered *"Hande hoch!"* Their hands went up and they trembled with fear. One of the pilots, who thought we were going to shoot them, began to cry. We took their pistols and belts and put them on our hips. In the closet we found some rifles and more pistols. After we collected all the weapons in the adjoining rooms, we told the pilots to put their hands down and enjoy their food. At that point in time, one of the pilots picked up a tray of cookies from the table and asked us to take some. We did and thanked him for the treat. After we tasted the cookies, the pilots relaxed and began to smile. I understood their smile as a smile of gratitude to us for treating them in a humane manner.

As we were enjoying the pilots' cookies, I looked into the hallway to see what was going on there. A number of our men walked this way and that way and one of them smoked two cigarettes at the same time. When I saw it, I could not contain my laughter.

Soon "Straceniec" joined us and brought with him a woman who, oblivious to what was happening around her, carried a tray of food for a couple of pilots who were constantly locked in one of the rooms on the third floor. When "Straceniec" inquired why the pilots were locked in, the woman replied that they operated a *Luftwaffe* (Air Force) radio station through which sensitive military information was being received and transmitted. Having learned this, "Straceniec" ordered the woman to carry on her duties as if nothing had happened. So she kept walking to the third floor and "Straceniec" followed her until they came to the door of the radio station room. There the woman knocked on the door and told the pilots that she brought their supper. One of the pilots opened the door and "Straceniec" forced his way into the room and pointed his pistol at the Germans who were there. Both of them were relaxed and wore tee-shirts. When they saw "Straceniec" with his gun, they were dumbfounded. When he ordered *"Hande hoch"*, one of them raised his hands

*Good evening, gentlemen.

quickly, but the other one looked like a zombie: his mouth wide open and his arms hanging helplessly. Only when "Straceniec" fired his pistol near the pilot's ear did he revive and raise his hands. At that time, "Blyskawica" joined "Straceniec" and both disarmed the pilots. When the pilots were deprived of their pistols, "Straceniec" disconnected the radio station. Then they searched the room and found more weapons. All told, they gained three pistols, two submachine guns, and three pairs of military boots.

After the Germans were disarmed on every floor, some of our men watched them while the rest of us were ordered to break into the rooms which were locked because their occupants were in town or on their furlough in Germany. The hatchets which we carried on our belts proved to be quite useful for this task. We chopped the doors above the locks and then two of us together shoved them with our shoulders until the doors gave in. The chopping of the doors and breaking of the locks caused a considerable noise. During this noisy period of our action, a German railroad police officer happened to walk by on the sidewalk in front of the building and heard the pounding. He came to "Iskra", who kept guard in front of the building, and asked him *"Was ist los?"* (What's the matter?) *"Ach, Scheisserei!"* (obscene expression) replied "Iskra". The officer scornfully waved his hand and said, "Yes, indeed." As soon as he turned around to resume his walk, "Iskra" put the barrel of his pistol to the officer's back and disarmed him. Then "Iskra" took him to the dining room where "Jach" was guarding the Germans. Since the officer's uniform was of a better quality than the one which "Iskra" was wearing, "Jach" advised him to trade with the officer. When "Iskra" accepted the suggestion, "Jach" took the guard duty in front of the building while "Iskra" changed uniforms and boots.

Our breaking into the unoccupied rooms yeilded five rifles, a great deal of ammunition, a number of uniforms, boots, sweaters, and blankets, and thirty knapsacks. By the time we finished our work, every one of us was loaded with pistols, rifles, and other military things which came in very useful in our struggle with the enemy.

"Cap", who carried his share of the German weapons, managed also to deprive the Germans of their medals, crosses, and other Nazi insignia. He enjoyed collecting such things.

After the door to the last unoccupied room gave in under the pressure of our shoulders and the weapons were taken, the captain ordered us to get ready to leave. As we began to leave the third floor, Captain "Kaktus" walked from room to room and told the Germans not to leave their rooms or start an alarm until one hour after our departure. He added that if any of them should try to leave the room before one hour, he would be shot. It appeared to me that neither the captain nor any of us trusted the Germans.

On the second floor, we found two or three Germans prostrated on the hallway floor. As we walked by, we avoided stepping on them. As we descended to the first floor, we saw more Germans on the corridor's floor. "Jach" told us that the ones who were on the floor had stayed on town too long and were late for dinner. "Iskra" disarmed them outside and "Jach" kept an eye on them inside the building.

As all of us who were inside gathered together on the corridor of the first floor, "Captain Kaktus" counted us and led us two by two across Opatowska Street toward the sidewalk on the edge of the city park. The machine gun crew and "Iskra" followed us. As soon as we reached the park, we left secure in the darkness of the night. The captain led us toward a vacant area full of small valleys behind the park, which was known as Piszczele. Before we managed to cross the city park, the Germans fired a flare. The sky became bright and we could hear the shouts of German soldiers who were stationed in various parts of the city. Then we heard the rumbling of motor vehicles and machine gun fire. The alarm was in full swing. The disarmed Germans did not keep their promise.

It appeared to me that in disarming the Germans we had overlooked a flare gun or one of our men who found it did not think it was worth taking since we had seized so many valuable weapons. After the first flare which started the alarm, many other flares burst in the sky in various sections of the city. The Germans sounded a general alarm. Fortunately, we were now out of their reach.

Quickening our pace, we entered the hollows of Piszczele in order to be lost in the darkness. From Piszczele, we headed through the fields in the direction of the village of Kobierniki. When we were in the midst of the fields, we noticed ahead of us a small light, as though from an oil lantern, which was moving away from us. At first, we paid no attention to this light, but when we heard the sound of a moving wagon from the direction of the light, we started to surmise that perhaps it could be a German army wagon riding into the area.

We were so enthusiastic as a result of our successful action that we did not want to pass up the opportunity to seize at least one more rifle or pistol. We all begged our captain to permit us to overtake the Germans and disarm them. The captain agreed and gave the order to quicken our march. Despite our tiredness and.the heavy load which each of us was carrying, we all got some new strength, a second wind, for the chase. After several minutes, we were not too far away from the wagon. Our guess was correct. This was a German military wagon. In a few more minutes, we would be beside the wagon, which we had already planned to use to transport our booty.

When we were taking a shortcut across the field in order to get ahead of the Germans, we heard German voices all around us here and there flashlights were blinking out signals. Immediately, we recognized that we were in the midst of German soldiers engaged in a military night training. Fortunately, we were near a row of willow trees growing along the side of the road. The branches of these trees were hanging to the ground, providing a perfect curtain. There we found a good hiding place. We hoped to avoid unnecessary shooting and perhaps even bloodshed; nevertheless, we were ready and prepared to fight if there was no other way out of the dangerous situation.

As soon as the nearest German flank passed us, ignoring the willows, we immediately started to withdraw from the area. The hilly terrain was our ally. After several minutes of an intensive and cautious march, we slipped away successfully from the Germans. We stopped finally beside a windmill in the neighboring village of Zurawica. There we obtained a wagon which caried our booty the rest of the way. After an hour's ride, we arrived at one of our secret quarters near Samborzec. After washing ourselves and taking some nourishment, we took a count of the German weapons. We were now in possession of many new-model rifles, pistols, ammunition, and uniforms. Since there was a unit of SS men in Samborzec, we decided to proceed to the manor of Jachimowice.

It was already morning when we arrived at our secret quarters at the manor of Jachimowice, owned by Mr. and Mrs. Bronikowsi. There we found a heartfelt welcome and rest, as well as pleasant companionship. From the manor of Jachimowice, we went to our quarters in Granicznik near Wiazownica. Our quarters there consisted of two adjacent farms which were on the end of a large forest.

As soon as we arrived in Granicznik, we kept examining our newly-acquired weapons. "Smigly", who had shot himself in the hand with a small-caliber lady's pistol, kept playing with the pistol from time to time. He was loading and reloading it over the dining room table. Some of us, including a ten-year-old farmer's son, were sitting about the table when "Smigly" introduced a round into the chamber and the pistol fired. The bullet hit the top of the heavy table under forty-five degrees angle, bounced off, and lodged itself in the boy's arm. All of us at the table got up with a great degree of anger at "Smigly" and his childish behavior that could have resulted in a death. One of our men who was near "Smigly" gently took the pistol from his trembling hand because there was a new round in its chamber. Our immediate superior, "Orlicz" (Stefan Franaszczuk), scolded "Smigly" and assigned him extra guard duty.

Then "Orlicz" asked for two volunteers to take the wounded boy to the physician's home in Osiek. "Straceniec" and I volunteered. Soon the farm wagon and horses were ready to go. We rode to Osiek as fast as the horses could go. It was late in the evening when we reached the physician's residence. He dutifully opened the door of his office and let us in. After examining the boy's arm, he told us that the bullet did not damage the bone nor any important blood vessel. It pierced the muscle and remained in it, under the skin, on the opposite side of its entry. The physician gave his patient a local anesthetic, disinfected the skin of his arm, cut the skin open over the bullet, and removed it with a great ease and skill. He gave the bullet to the boy as a memento. We offered to pay for the surgery, but the physician refused to take anything. The boy's wound, inflicted by a stray bullet, healed very fast and painlessly.

Upon a further examination of the small-caliber pistol, we discovered that its trigger mechanism was defective. This fact alleviated "Smigly's" guilt feelings. After a few days of rest and military lectures, we went out for our next action in Szczucin, where we expected to seize a tremendous quantity of arms and ammunition. This action, however, ended differently than that in Sandomierz.

## Chapter II

# Our Lady of Exiles Saved My Life

After disarming the Germans at 18 Mickiewicza Street in Sandomierz on November 12, 1943, our flying commando unit began preparations for another attack on the enemy. This time, our leaders decided to attack a post of the *Wehrmacht* (Army) soldiers who guarded the Szczucin Bridge on the Vistula River. According to the intelligence Captain "Kaktus" received a couple of days before the attack, twenty-four German soldiers were stationed in the guardhouse near the bridge on the right (eastern) side of the river. Their guardhouse was fortified by an earth rampart which had a small gate. The windows of the guardhouse were covered with an anti-hand grenade screen. The soldiers stationed in the guardhouse were armed with pistols, rifles, hand grenades, a few submachine guns, and a couple of machine guns. Four soldiers were always on guard duty. One pair guarded the bridge on the eastern side of the Vistula and the other on the western side. The soldiers on guard duty were armed with rifles and pistols.

The purpose of our attack was to disarm the *Wehrmacht* soldiers on the bridge and in the guardhouse and thus secure weapons and ammunition to be used in our struggle against the enemy.

A few days before our attack on the *Wehrmacht* post, a devout Catholic woman gave each of us in our unit a picture of Our Lady of Exiles and assured us that we would find it comforting in moments of danger. I put the picture of Our Lady in my wallet and carried it with me wherever I went.

During the Nazi occupation and the uprooting of Poles from the territories of Poland annexed to the German Reich, someone had conceived the idea of portraying the Blessed Virgin Mary as Our Lady of Exiles. The artist's painting was reproduced as a small holy picture and distributed primarily among those persons who were dispossessed and exiled. Such a picture gave strength and perseverance to the Polish exiles, who learned to believe that Blessed Virgin Mary, Mother of Christ, was present among them in their misery as their Mother and Protectress.

The preparations for the attack were nearing completion and we were waiting impatiently for the zero hour. Finally, the awaited moment arrived. Our hearts beat faster and more excitedly. After our last successful venture, everyone was full of optimism. Captain "Kaktus" assigned eighteen of us to take part in the attack, and each of us was given a specific function in it. The captain also selected the manor of Ruszcza as the place of our assembly in case we should be dispersed during the attack on the enemy.

On Friday, November 19, 1943, exactly one week after our previous attack on Sandomierz, we left our quarters in the manor of Beszyce in two large farm wagons and headed toward the Szczucin Bridge. For the sake of safety, Captain "Kaktus" rode on horseback ahead of our wagons. As we rode, the fall mud splattered about us under the pressure of the horses' hoofs and wagon wheels and the cool November air penetrated our bodies to the bone. When we arrived near the town of Rytwiany, we deviated from the main road to avoid it because there was a post of German police (Gendarmerie). After we passed by Rytwiany, we proceeded toward Lubnice. When we reached the vicinity of Lubnice, we left our wagons and horses there under the watchful eye of "Iskra" (Arkadiusz Swiercz) and "Mat" (Jerzy Kurczyk).

According to the captain's plan, we were to return to our wagons and horses by train after disarming the German post at the bridge. Having instructed "Iskra" and "Mat" to keep the horses and wagons in readiness for our return with the German arms, the captain led us to the railroad station in Lubnice. There, in accordance with our plan, we were to catch a train for Szczucin. After reaching the railroad station and waiting for a while, we discovered that the schedule for the arrivals and departures of the trains had been changed. Instead of waiting for the train without having the slightest idea when it would arrive, we decided to walk the railroad track toward Szczucin.

After walking for a few miles, we heard the familiar

sound of the locomotive behind us. We stopped and waited. Most of us had had enough of walking on the track. As the train came closer, we took our positions on each side of the track and one of our men who had a red flashlight attempted to stop it. It appeared that the engineer ignored the red light and kept going. At that moment, "Jach" (Wlodzimierz Gruszczynski) ran into the middle of the track and, with both of his hands, raised his rifle horizontally above his head. This time the engineer understood the signal and stopped the train.

As soon as the train stopped, the passengers, curious and frightened, opened the windows of the cars to see what had caused the stoppage of the train. At the same time, "Orzel" (Leon Siatrak) and "Pikolo" (Jan Szpakiewicz), with a light machine gun, entered the locomotive cab. The rest of us, dressed as German Air Force men and railroad policemen, entered the cars. As soon as we boarded the train, it continued to roll toward Szczucin. The passengers with whom we shared the cars soon discovered that we were not Germans but their own "boys from the forest". They were very friendly and well-disposed toward us.

Soon the train began to slow down. The Szczucin railroad bridge was near. As the locomotive approached the bridge, the engineer slowed the train even more. As our car approached the entrance to the bridge, "Jach" (Wlodzimierz Gruszczynski) and "Straceniec" (Jan Osemlak) jumped out from the car to disarm the first pair of guards. Ahead of them, near the bridge, they saw in the dim light two German guards who were standing near the tracks and watching the train. "Jach" and "Straceniec" approached the guards very briskly in military fashion. The guards stood at attention, expecting to be greeted by fellow Germans. Instead of the customary greeting, however, "Jach" and "Straceniec" pointed their pistols at them and ordered *"Hande hoch!"* The guards had no trouble raising their hands because their rifles were hanging on their shoulders. They were caught by total surprise. The soldier whom "Straceniec" ordered to raise his hands gave up his rifle without any resistance. But the one whom "Jach" approached raised his hands tardily and refused to give "Jach" his rifle. "Jach" became angry. He pushed the barrel of his pistol into the guard's abdomen and said to him in German, *"Was wollen Sie: Leben oder Tot?"* (Do you want to live or die?) This worked very effectively. The guard became panicky and let "Jach" take his rifle without any trouble.

As our car was passing by the entrance to the bridge, I saw the guards with their hands up and was encouraged by the successful disarming. Now one of our men and I were ready to jump out of our car and disarm two other guards on the other end of the bridge. As the train approached the other bank of the Vistula river, my companion and I noticed that the guards were not together as usual; instead, each of them stood *vis-a-vis* on opposite sides of the tracks. At the last moment, we had to change our plan of action. We quickly decided that my companion would disarm the guard on the left side of the train and I would take care of the guard on the right side. Soon we jumped from the car at the same time. In a moment, the train stopped and its cars separated us. I could not see what happened on the left side of the train. It appeared to me that my companion disarmed the guard without any problem.

The guard on my side of the train was tall and appeared to be about forty-years old. He wore a long winter coat with its collar up and military earmuffs that covered not only his ears but also a part of his face. As I walked toward him, he observed me very intently. His rifle was hanging from his left shoulder and his right hand was on the level of his chest, hidden under the winter coat. When I pointed the barrel of my rifle at him and shouted *"Hande hoch"*, he began to raise his left hand, but at the same time his right hand pulled out, with the speed of lightning, a pistol from behind his coat and began to fire at me. I squeezed the trigger of my rifle and fired at him. He stopped firing, stood on his feet for a short time, and then fell to the ground and rolled down the slope of the ramp. I tried to reload my rifle, but the casing of my first round was stuck in the chamber and the extractor stripped the rim of the casing. My Mauser rifle was reconditioned and there was a little pit, caused by rust, in its chamber. I had no cleaning rod in my rifle so there was no way to remove the empty casing. Now my small-caliber pistol and two hand grenades were my only weapons.

As a result of the guard's pistol shots and my rifle fire, pandemonium broke out. Our men began to fire at the guardhouse, and the Germans who were in it opened fire with everything they had: machine guns, submachine guns, rifles, hand grenades, and flares.

When some German soldiers came out of their fortified guardhouse to fire at Captain "Kaktus" (Tadeusz Strus),

"Blyskawica" (Boleslaw Szelong), and "Cap" (Marian Gaj), who began to move toward the gate of the guardhouse, "Orzel" (Leon Siatrak) and "Pikolo" (Jan Szpakiewicz), who were with the light machine gun on the locomotive, opened fire at the Germans. When the Germans returned their fire toward the locomotive, the machine gun crew left the locomotive and took a position on the ground. The clever engineer took advantage of this and pulled the train out of the battle zone.

The fire of our light machine gun and a small group of our men under the leadership of Captain "Kaktus" near the gate of the rampart made the Germans barricade the door to the guardhouse. The German soldiers who remained outside became victims of our machine gun and submachine gun bullets. Then Captian "Kaktus", "Blyskawica", and "Cap" went through the gate of the rampart and came close to the guardhouse. In order to subdue the fire from within the guardhouse, the captain kept firing his German submachine gun (*Machinen Pistole*) at the windows. At the same time, "Blyskawica" used his rifle to remove the screen in the windows which protected the Germans from hand grenades. He was convinced that only our hand grenades could smoke out the soldiers from the guardhouse. "Cap" was aiding "Blyskawica" in his task, and "Piorun" (Kazimierz Stobinski), who happened to be near the gate, began to shout, in the German language, the summons of surrender: *"Soldaten ergeben Sie sich!"*

After disarming the guards on the left side of the Vistula River, "Jach" and "Straceniec" walked over the bridge to the right side, where our attack was about to commence. They were in the middle of the bridge when the first shots were fired. At that moment, they shot the guards, pushed their bodies into the river, and ran toward the battle. After they arrived there, they took firing positions and began to fire into the windows of the guardhouse. In the meantime, the submachine gun with which the captain fired so effectively at the windows of the guardhouse jammed. As he was attempting to fix it, a German hand grenade which we called a "potato masher" landed near him and exploded. As a result of the explosion, the captain sustained a wound on his forehead and "Cap" lost his eye. Blood covered their eyes and faces. They could not see. With the help of others, the two men began to withdraw toward the bridge.

There was still a chance of taking the guardhouse, but

the German units which were stationed in Szczucin and in the neighboring towns were already alerted and getting ready to help their comrades near the bridge. As a matter of fact, we could hear the sound of their sirens. The key to our success was an element of surprise and quiet disarmament of the guards at the bridge and in the guardhouse. We had lost the element of surprise and we did not have enough time to take by force the fortified guardhouse. Therefore, after a short consultation with "Orlicz" (Stefan Franaszczuk), who was next in command, Captain "Kaktus" said, "Boys, let us retreat." As a result of the captain's decision, all our men near the guardhouse began to withdraw toward the entrance of the bridge. Those who were not wounded helped the captain and "Cap".

When our men, under the leadership of Captain "Kaktus", began to withdraw from the area around the guardhouse, "Orzel" and "Pikolo", with their machine gun, had now their firing position at the railroad tracks. Their position was the farthest from the bridge. My position was somewhere between their position and the entrance to the bridge. There I was, lying on the railroad ramp, pinned to the ground by German tracer bullets which were coming from the guardhouse. For all practical purposes, my jammed rifle was useless, and the small-caliber pistol which I carried was insufficient against the powerful weapons of the Germans. Since the body of the guard whom I shot had rolled down the slope of the ramp under a complicated network of barbed wire, it did not occur to me to retrieve the guard's rifle whenever the enemy's flares illuminated the area.

When our men began to withdraw from the guardhouse area, the German fire intensified toward the ramp. A number of times, I crawled toward the top of the ramp and near the railroad tracks to see what was happening. But each time, the enemy's machine gun fire forced me to take cover behind the steel of the tracks and the dirt of the ramp. As I crawled the ramp for the last time, all our men were already on the bridge and the Germans began to come out of the guardhouse to fire at them. Soon the Germans came near the entrance of the bridge and kept firing at our men, who were already close to its western end. Enemy bullets wounded "Sep" (Edward Stawiarz) and "Zbik", who walked close to each other. Both of them were hit in one of their arms. Then "Blyskawica" was seriously wounded.

The bullet pierced his rib cage and penetrated his chest cavity on the right side. Immediately, he began to lose strength and experienced a choking sensation and an oppressive feeling in his chest. He no longer could walk. In order not to slow the retreat, he pulled out his pistol and attempted to shoot himself. Two of our men took the pistol from his hand.

It was too late for me to follow my companions. My chance of crossing the bridge was gone. Therefore, I decided to swim across the Vistula River under the bridge. All of a sudden, my left ear began to burn. When I touched it, I felt sticky blood on my fingers. Obviously, during my efforts to disarm the guard, his bullet had come close to my head. In order to reach the bank of the river, I had to crawl under a network of barbed wire which the Germans had installed. After doing this, I entered the water and began to cross the river. At first, the water was rather shallow and I managed to reach the first pier of the bridge. Encouraged by my initial success, I continued walking toward the second pier. The water was getting deeper and deeper but I still felt ground under my feet as I came to the second pier.

As I walked between the second and the third pier, I lost the bottom of the river and began to swim. The weight of my jammed rifle became an obstacle in swimming so I let it go to the bottom. In my knapsack, I carried five kilograms of explosives. I could not use my hands for anything but swimming, however; therefore, I did not make any attempt to remove it. My winter coat and military boots interfered more and more with the free movement of my arms and legs. The river's current, which became stronger now, began to carry me away from the bridge. The bright light from German flares illuminated the river and the bridge. Some of the Germans were already on the bridge. They must have noticed me, because a series of bullets splashed near me. When the Germans fired their next flare, I attempted to swim under the water. With each new flare, I did the same thing a number of times.

I was losing my strength and taking in water. The Germans kept firing at me. I began to lose hope of saving my life. I became terrified. At the same time, death appeared to me as a liberating factor. I began sinking deeper and deeper. I was drowning. A thought came to my mind that my life was rapidly coming to an end. From all appearances, there was no hope. I regretted the fact that I would die at such an early age. The most important events of my life flashed in my mind as if projected on a movie screen. Fear of death left me and; in fact, I experienced a blissful feeling. In what might have been the last moment of my life, I remembered the pious woman who gave me a picture of Our Lady of Exiles and assured me of her prayers. In fact, I had the picture on me in my pocketbook. My heart started to beat rapidly and the words of prayer came to my mind, "Mary, Mother of God, pray for me...help me...", I prayed.

Suddenly something happened to me. Some force, as it were, lifted me from the bottom of the Vistula. A new strength entered my body. With all my might, I began to swim again. As I moved my legs with a new energy, my military boots came off. Relieved of them, I continued swimming with the current, farther and farther from the bridge and the Germans, who upon seeing my struggles in the water must have assumed that I had drowned. Since swimming on my back was easy for me, I turned on my back and let the current carry me. After a while, I tested the depth of the river and was surprised when my feet touched bottom.

I walked toward something which looked to me like a small island and reached its shore. It was wonderful to be on land again. I thought of resting there for a moment and then making an attempt to reach the real shore of the Vistula. But as I walked farther, I discovered a path which fishermen must have made. I followed the path and came to the realization that I was not on an island. It was a piece of land in the shape of a peninsula. I was pleasantly surprised and kept walking away from the river.

Momentarily, I deviated from the path and walked into a place where basket makers cut, near the ground, young willow twigs. I wounded my feet on the sharp stubs. In order to examine my feet, I removed my socks and threw them away; they were wet and muddy. From that point on, I walked barefooted. Since the ground was freezing, my feet became numb and I felt no pain in them anymore.

The frosty air and my wet clothing made me accelerate my walk to stay warm. Soon I reached a system of dikes which were built along the river to prevent floods. I began to proceed in the direction of Polaniec.

The shooting stopped for a moment, only to resume again away from the bridge. I wondered whether the Germans had caught up with our men, resulting in the exchange of fire. Actually, a detachment of Germans which was rushing to aid the unit at the bridge opened fire on the Germans who pursued our group. In the darkness of the night, it took the Germans some time to discover their mistake. In the meantime, our men gained a safe distance from the enemy.

After an hour's walk along the dike, I noticed a distant light which looked like that of a naphtha lamp placed near the window in somebody's home. Since I was in need of dry clothes and shoes, I decided to walk toward the light hoping to find some help from the people who possibly lived there. When I came close to the light, it became clear to me that it was indeed coming from the window of a house which was somewhat distant from the other houses in the village. As I cautiously approached the house, the light in the window went out. I went to the window and tapped on it lightly. No one responded. In a hushed voice, I said, "Please let me in. I am a partisan, a Polish soldier. I need your help." Again, no one answered. I tapped on the window again, this time with a greater perseverance and loudness. A woman answered and said, "Sir, I am afraid to let you in. Please go somewhere else." I intended to plead further with the woman, but a window opened in another part of the house and an older man appeared in it and said, "I will let you in, sir; please come to my door. I am an old legionnaire and I understand." Immediately, he opened the door to his part of the house and let me come in. His wife was also on her feet and ready to help. Both of them were extremely hospitable and helpful. They helped me take off my wet clothing, took care of my minor wounds, and told me to warm up in their bed.

My wounds were superficial. The bullet from the pistol of the German whom I had attempted to disarm had nipped my right ear, fragments of hand grenades or bullets had lacerated my left buttock in two places, and barbed wire had cut skin on both of my hands.

While I was getting warmed in the couple's bed, the legionnaire went to his wardrobe to procure some clothing and shoes for me. At the same time, his wife boiled a pot of milk to keep me warm from within. After drinking a couple of cups of hot milk, I felt well enough to be on my way. I dressed, put my pistol and hand grenades on my belt and my knapsack with explosives on my back, and was ready to go to Polaniec, where my relatives lived. My hosts felt that I should not walk to Polaniec, however, because the Germans were alerted and probably watched the roads. The legionnaire offered to take me to his relative's secluded farmhouse, where I could stay for a couple of days. He told me that his cousin was a member of a local post of the Home Army and could easily get me in touch with my group. I accepted his offer and soon we were riding in his farm wagon to the secluded farm. It was almost morning when we reached the farm.

The farmhouse was indeed secluded and far away from any road. The farmer, his wife, and their red-haired teenage daughter were as hospitable as the legionnaire and his wife. After a short conversation, they offered me the warmest bedroom and advised me to take a rest. They stayed up and did their morning chores. In spite of my most dramatic experiences at the Szczucin Bridge, I fell asleep and did not wake until noon. As I woke up, an aroma of chicken soup ingredients filled the farmhouse. The lady of the house and her daughter were preparing a fine chicken dinner which usually farmers' wives serve only on Sundays.

During the meal, the farmer told me that he had reported my presence in his home to the commandant of the local Home Army post and the commandant was expected to arrive at any moment to see me. The commandant arrived in the afternoon and provided a farm wagon which took me to his subordinates in Polaniec. I was very grateful to both farm families and the local commandant for the wonderful help they offered me in my moments of extreme need. By helping me to save my life, they endangered their own lives and the lives of their dear ones.

When I was swimming across the Vistula River and walking to the farmhouse for help, the majority of our men under the leadership of Captain "Kaktus", having gone over the bridge, walked into the fields near the railroad tracks. The fields were full of thorns and briers. Fortunately, the thorns and briers grew only in the vicinity of the railroad tracks. As they went futher, they entered cultivated fields in which both walking and carrying the wounded were much easier. Soon they came to a meadow, where Captain "Kaktus" ordered a short stop and asked for a bandage for his wounded forehead. "Jach" offered his bandage to the captain and dressed his wound.

After his wound was properly dressed, the captain reorganized the group. He assigned some men to take care of those who were seriously wounded, appointed a couple of scouts, and pointed out the direction in which the group was to proceed. At the same time, he sent one of the men to the drivers of the farm wagons which we had left in the forest near the railroad station of Lubnice. They were ordered to drive the wagons to the manor of Ruszcza near Polaniec, which according to our original plan was to be the gathering point of the group in case of dispersion.

After walking a while through the farmland, the group came to a farm. The captain hoped to get a team of horses there and a farm wagon to carry the wounded. When the farmer was bringing his horses out of the barn to hitch them to the wagon, a couple of German military personnel carriers appeared on the road near the farmhouse and stopped there. When the soldiers came out of the trucks, Captain "Kaktus" ordered his men to withdraw from the farmyard into the adjacent field. As they were pulling out into the field, the scaling of the fence proved to be somewhat difficult and noisy. The Germans on the road must have heard the noise because they fired a couple of flares to illuminate the field. However, a heavy fog protected our men from the eyes of the soldiers. At the same time, the fog which covered the whole area hindered orientation in the terrain.

After getting away from the farm, the captain became disoriented and asked his men for suggestions on which direction to proceed. "Jach" was the first one to speak. He said, "Captain, the Germans are behind us, to the right of us and to the left we can hear the barking of the dogs; only in the front of us seems to be quiet and safe.* Since no one in the group had better advice, the captain asked "Jach" to lead. "Jach" stepped in front of the group and asked everybody to follow him.

As the group walked behind "Jach", the German flares illuminated the area from time to time. Each time a flare appeared in the sky, they all hit the ground and then walked again. After a while of marching in such a way, "Jach" discovered that he had lost the group which followed him. He obviously overestimated the speed with which the group could proceed with the wounded and got so far ahead of the group that he lost contact with it. He went back in search of the group but did not find it so he resumed his walk in the previous direction.

*Wlodzimerz Gruszczynski, *Lotna Sandomierska* (Kielce-Warszawa) p. 92.

The wet soil of the farm fields made his walk very difficult. On his boots he carried loads of heavy mud. He was getting tired and needed rest. After dragging his feet for a while, "Jach" could hear the barking of dogs. This indicated that there was a village nearby. He decided to go in the direction from which came the sound of the dogs' barking. After walking for a while, farm buildings emerged from the heavy fog. "Jach" cautiously entered the farmyard and noticed that there was a pile of logs. The logs were somewhat elevated from the ground. Since the dogs in the neighborhood began to bark rather violently, "Jach" crawled under the logs. Soon a group of German soldiers entered the farmyard. With their flashlights, they explored the area. "Jach" buried his wallet in which he kept his identification card, driver's license, etc., in the mud. He removed his pistol from the holster to end his life if the Germans discovered him.

After a while, the soldiers left the yard. They went to search the neighboring farm buildings. As soon as they left, "Jach" rushed to the barn and buried himself in the straw. Soon he fell asleep and slept until a couple of farmers came to the barn and began the work of thrashing. When he came out of the pile of straw, the farmers were greatly astonished. After "Jach" explained to them who he was and why he was in the barn, the owner of the farm invited him to the farmhouse. There, the farmer's wife gave him water to wash with and a warm breakfast. Then she asked him to stay in the house and rest for a few hours. Having rested, "Jach" took the shortest and safest road to Polaniec.

In Polaniec, I met Kazimerz Jarzyna and a couple of other members of the Home Army. They invited me to their favorite restaurant, where we celebrated our acquaintance with some cold cuts and whiskey. They were very interested in my unusual experiences at the bridge and asked me to tell and retell some of the highlights. They told me that the men of my group took horses and wagons in Ruszcza near Polaniec to carry their wounded in the direction of Osiek. Soon "Jach" and "Piorun" came also to Polaniec.

The local Home Army men transferred us by means of horse and buggy to our quarters in the old manor of Ruszcza near Sulislawice.

I did not realize until we arrived at the grounds of the manor of Ruszcza that I was supposed to be dead. A man who was on guard duty expressed great surprise at the sight of me. Reflecting the belief of others, he told me that everybody took for granted that I was killed by the Germans at the bridge. Some men in the group were convinced that they saw me on the ground dead or mortally wounded. So when we entered the manor house, there were more expressions of surprise, shouts of joy, and fraternal hugs. Soon I was struck by the absence of "Cap", "Blyskawica", "Zbik", and "Sep". All four of them were wounded and hospitalized at the Holy Ghost Hospital in Sandomierz. Captain "Kaktus", with a bandage on his forehead, was on his feet to greet us. He was already planning a new attack on the enemy.

During my conversation with my comrads-in-arms, I learned that "Orzel" and "Pikolo", who manned the machine gun, were also unable to withdraw over the bridge. However, they did not attempt to swim across the Vistula River. They walked on its right side until they found a boatman who took them to the other side of the river. They returned to the unit unharmed.

As is true in any failure, our failure at the Szczucin Bridge had a cause: a lack of coordination of our group's activities with other partisan groups in the area of Szczucin. Now we became aware that a few hours before our attack on the Germans at the bridge, another guerrilla group, not knowing of our plans, roused the Germans, who then instead of sleeping in the barracks as usual waited for an attack in full military readiness.

## Chapter III

# We Fly to Thy Protection

In the southern part of the District of Sandomierz and not too far from the town of Polaniec, which was made famous by the Kosciuszko's Manifesto (May 7, 1794), there is the small village of Struzki. On its north side it borders with the large and well-established village of Osala, and on its southeast side lies the historical village of Tursko. The village of Struzki belongs to the Parish of Niekrasow, which boasts of its ancient and beautiful wooden church.

During World War II, the residents of Struzki were rather poor and earned their livelihood by tilling small and sandy farms and working as loggers in the nearby forest. Their homes and farm buildings were small and covered with straw roofs. The central point of the village was the community building, which housed not only community offices but also a local grade school. The road which linked the village with the outside world ran on its western side from the north to the south. The northern part of the road connected Struzki with Osiek and the southern part with Polaniec.

When shortly before the outbreak of World War II the government began the construction of a highway from Osiek to Polaniec, many residents of Struzki found employment close to home. Even though the highway was not completed before September 1, 1939, the village of Struzki nevertheless gained some recognition as being in the middle between these two towns.

The war activities of 1939 did not greatly disturb the life of this peaceful village. The Polish as well as the German armies bypassed the area of Struzki due to the lack of good roads. The people of the village were happy about this, and after three years of Nazi occupation, they hoped and prayed they would remain safe to the end of the World War II hostilities. Unfortunately, they underestimated the barbarism of Hitler's evil empire.

For some time already, a unit of the Nazi Gendarmerie which was stationed in the town of Rytwiany terrorized the population of the whole area. Under the guise of requisition (foraging) of food, pigs, and poultry, they beat farmers and shot those who attempted to run away from them. They engaged in plain robbery and murder of innocent people.

In order to curb such criminal behavior, six members of the "Jedrus" commando unit decided to eliminate without a trace the Nazi "foraging expedition". With this purpose in mind, they prepared in a hurry an ambush on the road which led from Struzki to Rytwiany on Wednesday, on June 2, 1943. Under the leadership of Stanislaw Wiacek ("Inspektor"), the members of the commando unit took their positions on the edge of the forest with a view of the road. Soon they discovered that their firing positions were not good enough. But they had no time to change; the Germans were coming. They were riding in two farm wagons. Unfortunately, the wagons were at a considerable distance from each other. There was a great need for more men and weapons to take care of both wagons at the same time.

Soon the first wagon, with three Germans and a Polish driver (Kalina), arrived on the scene. "Inspektor" shouted "Fire!" The machine gun fire killed the driver and the German officer in charge and wounded two German gendarmes. The wounded gendarmes managed to escape into the forest. The horses, frightened by the gun fire, carried the corpses away. In the meantime, the second wagon came to a halt and the Germans jumped down from it, took firing positions, and began to fire. During the exchange of violent gun fire, one German was killed, another (Von Tutze) surrendered, and the third managed to escape. Those who escaped returned to their post in Rytwiany and reported the attack.

The day after the attack, Thursday, June 3, 1943, which was the Feast of the Ascension of Our Lord, the people of Struzki were getting up and dressing for the early Mass when somebody reported the sound of many motor vehicles. Soon twenty-three black trucks appeared on the road.* They carried SS men

*In addition to the trucks, there was also a number of smaller motor vehicles.

and Gendarmerie.* Besides the SS men and Gendarmerie who came in the military trucks, there were also members of *Wehrmacht* who were on furlough in the area of Sandomierz and *Hitlerjugend* from German settlements of Luszyca, Mikolajow, Przeczow, Mokoszyn, Gerlachow, and Chwalki. The trucks halted on the road in front of the community building. The Germans came out of their trucks, armed with machine guns, submachine guns, rifles, and hand grenades. They also brought with them a couple of small-caliber cannons.

As soon as the Germans surrounded the village, they opened fire about 6:00 a.m. At first there was one pistol or rifle shot. Then they began to fire the small-caliber cannons from the vicinity of the community building.** The shells of the cannons started fires in the farmhouses and other farm buildings; they were incendiary shells. When fire began to gut the building, the people attempted to save their property as much as they could. The Germans did not allow them to do so and shot them as soon as they came out of their houses. Those who were not shot in front of their houses were forced to go inside to burn alive. Children who ran outside of their homes were caught by the Nazi "supermen" and thrown into the flames.

The SS men did not spare even a woman who had just given birth to a child; they burned both of them. The elderly and sick persons were given the same treatment. In the Nowicki house, there was the body of Ignacy Nowicki in a casket ready to be buried on Friday, June 4. The Nazi barbarians did not respect the sacredness of the human body; they opened the casket, threw the body out, and burned the house with the widow in it. The perverted Hitlerites tortured the children of Wincenty and Wladyslawa Bobek: Natalia, four, Wieslaw, three, and Teresa, six months. Then they threw them into the flames of their house, where they burned alive together with their parents.

One of the Nazi criminals pierced with his bayonet the six-year-old daughter of Ludwik and Stanislawa Drozdz and

*According to Piotr (Marian) Sierant, the core of the German force constituted 3rd Company of 1st Battalion, which was a part of the 17th Regiment of the SS. See his work entitled *Drugi Pulk Piechoty Legionow Armii krajowej* (manuscript).

**Piotr Sierant, "Hitlerowska Pacifikacja Wsi Struzki" (Wybor Prac Na Konkurs Imienia Jozefa Wyrwy, London 1977) p. 84-85.

threw her into the flames. When she was being consumed by the fire, he also pushed her bewildered parents into the flames.

As the Nazi "supermen" came to the farmhouse of the Strzelecki family, they found fifty-year-old Jan Strzelecki holding in his arms two of his one-year-old grandchildren, Leon Tworek and Anna Wieruszewski. In the house were two of Jan Strzelecki's daughters, Eleanor Tworek, the mother of one of the children, and her sister, Helena Strzelecki. The murderers first wounded Helena, then set fire to the house and threw both sisters into the fire. Then they took Jan Strzelecki away from his burning house and killed him while he was still holding his grandchildren in his arms. After he fell to the ground, the Nazi beasts smashed the heads of the infants with the butts of their rifles.

On the road nearby, the Nazis apprehended twenty-year-old Wladyslawa Kurgan from Luszyca, who was on the way to visit her relatives in Struzki. They tortured her first and then shot her in the chest. On the edge of the forest, the vicious criminals found four women: Waleria Salat, forty, Maria Sztucinska, forty-seven, Helena Sztucinska, sixteen, and Jozefa Wnuk, seventeen. They brought them to the front of the community building and killed them in front of about thirty officers.*

Some of the younger residents attempted to save themselves by running away, but almost every one of them was killed by the bullets of the Germans, who constituted a cordon around the village. Only a very few persons managed to escape into the forest or into the already tall rye which grew abundantly in the fields along the edge of the village.

Eight members of the "Jedrus" commando unit, under the leadership of Jozef Wiacek ("Sowa"), attempted to save the village of Struzki from total annihilation. They attacked the Germans with a heavy machine gun, two light machine guns, and rifles, killing about forty of them. Although they had to withdraw because of the overwhelming numerical strength of the enemy and the superiority of the enemy's weapons, their attack nevertheless created a considerable disorder in the ranks of the Germans and thus facilitated the escape of some of the villagers. By the time the "Jedrus" men were forced to withdraw, most of the buildings in the village were in flames.

*Piotr Sierant, "Hitlerowska Pacyfikacja Wsi Struzki," *loco cit.*

At the same time, the Nazi arsonists and murderers approached the fence of the Izbinski farm buildings, where an unusual occurrence took place which finally led to saving the lives of the entire family.

The heroine of the occurrence was seventeen-year-old Maria Izbinski, who was at home at the time. Both of her parents and three of her sisters were also at home. Her fourth sister, nine-year-old Zofia, was able to escape from the village before the Germans surrounded it.

When Maria saw the approaching SS men, she started to look for a hiding place. At first, she ran into the house, but there she was overcome with a greater fear since she realized what had happened to the other houses in the village. Then she thought about hiding in the dugout built in the garden for storing potatoes in the winter and milk in the summer. As she was leaving the house, her eyes rested on the picture of Our Lady of Czestochowa that was hanging on the wall, which her mother had bought in Warsaw about one month before this fateful day. The moment Maria's eyes rested on the picture of Our Lady, she was immediately struck with the thought, "I shall take the picture and I shall be saved." She went to the wall and with trembling hands took hold of the picture. Then, holding the picture before her like a shield, she went out to meet the approaching SS men, reciting in a loud voice the words of the popular antiphon, "We fly unto Thy protection oh Holy Mother of God..."

When Maria stepped out into the garden, the SS men, with weapons ready to fire, had begun to approach the fences of the farmyard. Some were coming through the gate; others were breaking the fences in order to get close to the farm buildings to set them afire. Those who were entering through the gate were bringing back Maria's father, who had attempted to escape on his horse. Kicking him and beating him with the butts of their rifles, the Germans were forcing him back into the house. Among the Germans who were entering the Izbinskis' farmyard was the commanding officer.

After they noticed Maria walking toward them with the picture of Our Lady, the Germans began to shout in Polish, "Throw the picture to the ground!" It appeared to Maria that the murderers were afraid of Our Lady's picture.

When the commanding officer saw Maria with Our Lady's picture and heard the words of her prayer, he stopped, lowered his submachine gun, and stood at attention as if rooted to the spot. When his subordinates wanted to shoot Maria's father, he did not allow it; when they attempted to set fire to the house, he forbade them. He ordered Maria's father and her sisters to climb onto the roofs of the house and the farmbuildings to protect them from catching fire from the fragments of burning roofs of the houses and barns in the immediate area. He himself went about the farmyard putting out fires in the straw which was lying around. Then he ordered his subordinates to search the Izbinski house and the farm buildings. The SS men made a thorough search but did not find anything incriminating, even though there were some weapons and ammunition hidden in one of the buildings.

When the search was completed, the commanding officer ordered his men to leave the Izbinskis' farmyard and go to the neighboring farmyard, which belonged to the Wnuk family. Being the last to leave, the commanding officer turned to Maria and her family and said, "You were very fortunate." Then he walked out through the gate, closed it, and followed his men, who were already engaged in murdering the Wnuks and burning their farm buildings.

Maria went back into the house and replaced the picture of Our Lady on the wall. She gathered some flowers in the garden and placed them before the picture. Deep in her heart, she knew that the Mother of Christ did not disregard her petitions, but delivered her and her whole family from the evil of cruel death.

By noon, the SS men had completed their bloody act of annihilation of Struzki. Upon leaving, they took with them the mayor of the village, Jan Salat, whom they killed later at the prison in Sandomierz. On the scene of the mass murder and destruction there remained the ashes of sixty persons who were burned alive, the bodies of seventeen persons who were shot and killed, and the ashes of most of the houses and farm buildings in the village.*

I witnessed the tragedy of Struzki from a distance of about two miles. My friends, with whom I was staying in

*The survivors reported that a soldier of the Wehrmacht, Heinrich Hesler, who was home on furlough in one of the German villages of the area, committed the most atrocious acts of barbarism in Struzki on that tragic day. See Piotr Sierant, *loc cit.*

Niekrasow, and I were awakened by the fire of the small-caliber German cannons and machine guns. We dressed in a hurry and walked through the fields toward the village of Struzki. From a safe distance, I could hear the shouting of the Nazi murderers and the voices of the victims. Our hearts were full of pain for the people of Struzki, and frustration on account of our impotence to help them in any way. We had only a few small-caliber pistols and a very limited amount of ammunition. After the SS men completed their demonic work and left the village of Struzki, we hesitated to go there for fear of their unexpected return. We spent most of the day in the fields and returned to Niekrasow for the night.

The following morning, I arrived on the scene of this horrible and inhuman tragedy. Smoke was still coming from the burned ruins and the air was filled with the odor of burned human bodies. I walked from one ruin to another in order to see as much as possible. I saw the scorched bodies of men and women with arms and legs burned away. I saw the bodies of little children shrunken to the size of a man's arm. Among the embers there were bodies of mothers surrounded by the charred bodies of their children. The villagers who succeeded in saving their lives were moving about, in a trance, among the smoldering ruins. They were alive, but they could just as well have been dead, seeing the murdered and burned members of their families. Some of them, in fact, went mad and attempted to throw themselves into the still-burning ruins.

After a few days, there was a mass funeral which was attended by thousands of people, not only from the Parish of Niekrasow but also from other parishes in the area. The local pastor, Father Jan Smigielski, and Father Jan Sroczynski conducted the funeral services. The funeral procession extended five-hundred meters in length. It was an overwhelming manifestation of patriotism. The coffins were draped with red and white flags, and seventeen huge wreaths made by the girls in the parish were carried in the procession to the cemetery.

When the remains of the murdered victims were lowered into the common grave, there was a deadly silence except for the sound of sobbing throughout the crowd. As soon as the gravediggers began to cover the coffins with the fresh soil, there was much weeping and lamenting, not only for those whose bodies were being buried but also for those who were still alive and yet subject to a similar fate at the hands of Nazi barbarians.

During my summer vaction in 1952, Father Jan Smigielski, who was still pastor of the Parish of Niekrasow, did me a great favor. He helped me find the heroine of this story, Maria Izbinski, who was married to a young man named Wawrzkiewicz. Maria and her husband lived, at that time, in the village of Pliskowola, which was in the Parish of Osiek. Father Smigielski and I met Maria in the fields, where she was tending her cows. She willingly told us the details of her unusual experiences on that tragic day in Struzki. She spoke slowly to give me a chance to take notes. From time to time she paused momentarily because her emotions and tears prevented her from talking. At times her body trembled and she cried like a child.

She ended the recounting of her experience with these words, "We are all convinced that the intercession of Our Lady of Czestochowa miraculously saved us from death. In gratitude for her intercession and protection, my father promised to build in our village a chapel in honor of the Blessed Mother of Christ so that each year on the anniversary of the burning of Struzki, Mass may be offered for the repose of the souls of the murdered villagers. My father died before he could fulfill his promise. He managed, however, to buy enough stones for the chapel. Now we, his children, have a sacred duty to complete his unfinished work."

Today the village of Struzki has been rebuilt. On the ruins of the burned buildings and on the ground soaked with the blood of innocent victims stand new houses and farm buildings and fruit trees and fields of wheat are growing. In the walls of many houses one can find some partially burned beams, the remains of the former buildings, reminding the present residents of the tragic events of bygone years.

List of the persons murdered by the Nazis in Struzki on June 3, 1943*

| Name | Parents' Names | Age | Residence |
|---|---|---|---|
| 1. Zofia Glica | Jozef & Marianna | 77, widow | Struzki |
| 2. Michalina Osinska | Unknown | 76 | Warsaw |
| 3. Michal Sztucinski | Wojeciech & Katarzyna | 76, married | Struzki |
| 4. Antoni Szkutnik | Jan & Maria | 73, widower | Struzki |
| 5.Wawrzyniec Bobek | Mateusz & Agnieszka | 70, widower | Struzki |
| 6. Jozefa Sztucinska | Daughter of Agnieszka | 67, widow | Struzki |

*Cf. Piotr Sierant, "Hitlerowska Pacifikacja Wsi Struzki" (Wybor Prac Na Konkurs Imienia Jozefa Wyrwy, London, 1977) pp. 96-97.

| | | | |
|---|---|---|---|
| 7. Katarzyna Gora | Kazimierz & Teofila | 65, widow | Struzki |
| 8. Agnieszka Wiecek | Jan & Katarzyna | 63, widow | Struzki |
| 9. Kazimierz Kasek | Andrzej & Tekla | 60, married | Struzki |
| 10. Jan Salat | Tomasz & Marianna | 50, married | Struzki |
| 11. Jan Strzelecki | Andrzej & Wiktoria | 50, married | Ossala |
| 12. Waleria Salat | Piotr & Anna | 49, married | Struzki |
| 13. Marianna Balicka | Wincenty & Zofia | 48, married | Struzki |
| 14. Jozefa Gasek | Jan & Franciszka | 47, married | Struzki |
| 15. Marianna Sztucinska | Jan & Jozefa | 47, married | Struzki |
| 16. Jadwiga Strzelecka | Aleksander & Eleonora | 47, married | Ossala |
| 17. Eleonora Kasek | Jozef & Marianna | 46, married | Struzki |
| 18. Wojciech Chmielowiec | Michal & Marianna | 45, married | Struzki |
| 19. Leon Spychala | Wawrzyniec & Katarzyna | 43, married | Struzki |
| 20. Antoni Wnuk | Michal & Antonina | 43, married | Struzki |
| 21. Stanislaw Spychala | Ignacy & Marianna | 40, married | Struzki |
| 22. Julianna Glica | Wojciech & Katarzyna | 39, married | Struzki |
| 23. Ludwick Drozdz | Jan & Marianna | 38, married | Tursko-Zagumnie |
| 24. Wladyslawa Gora | Tomasz & Franciszka | 38, married | Strukzi |
| 25. Staniskawa Drozdz | Wojciech & Agnieszka | 37, married | Tursko-Zagumnie |
| 26. Janina Ostrowska | Ludwik & Michalina | 36 | Warsaw |
| 27. Stanislawa Nowicka | Wojciech & Maria | 35, married | Struzki |
| 28. Katarzyna Wnuk | Walenty & Katarzyna | 35, married | Struzki |
| 29. Jan Glica | Mikolaj & Franciszka | 35, married | Tursko-Zagumnie |
| 30. Stefiania Wiacek | Wladyslaw & Marianna | 32, married | Struzki |
| 31. Wladyslaw Wos | Walenty & Marianna | 31, bachelor | Tursko-Zagumnie |
| 32. Wincenty Bobek | Wawrzyniec & Maria | 30, married | Struzki |
| 33. Feliks Niedzwiecki | Szymon & Jozefa | 30, bachelor | Luszyca |
| 34. Wladyslawa Bobek | Andrzej & Katarzyna | 28, married | Struzki |
| 35. Stanislawa Chmielowiec | Michal & Zofia | 27, married | Struzki |
| 36. Marianna Durma | Wojciech & Marianna | 27, maiden | Tursko-Zagumnie |
| 37. Mieczyslaw Jakubik | Stanislaw & Agnieszka | 27, married | Struzki |
| 38. Marianna Wos | Walenty & Katarzyna | 27, widow | Struzki |
| 39. Tadeusz Gora | Wojciech & Katarzyna | 25, bachelor | Struzki |
| 40. Sabina Szkutnik | Boleslaw & Maria | 25, married | Struzki |
| 41. Honorata Steborowska | Jozef & Jozefa | 23, married | Struzki |
| 42. Zofia Salat | Jan & Waleria | 20, maiden | Struzki |
| 43. Eleonora Tworek | Jan & Jadwiga | 20, married | Ossala |
| 44. Czeslawa Jakubik | Leon & Stanislawa | 17, married | Struzki |
| 45. Helena Strzelecka | Jan & Jadwiga | 17, maiden | Ossala |
| 46. Jozefa Wnuk | Antoni & Helena | 17, maiden | Struzki |
| 47. Jan Wos | Jan & Anna | 17, bachelor | Struzki |
| 48. Wladyslawa Kasek | Kazimierz & Eleonora | 16, maiden | Struzki |
| 49. Helena Sztucinska | Jan & Marianna | 16, maiden | Struzki |
| 50. Jozef Gasek | Jozef & Jozefa | 13, boy | Struzki |
| 51. Eleonora Burcza | Daughter of Stanislawa | 12, girl | Struzki |
| 52. Marianna Spychala | Leon & Stanislawa | 12, girl | Struzki |
| 53. Janina Wnuk | Antoni & Wincentyna | 10, girl | Struzki |
| 54. Zofia Kasek | Kazimierz & Elenora | 10, girl | Struzki |
| 55. Janina Ostrowska | Henryk & Janina | 10, girl | Warsaw |
| 56. Wojciech Skucinski | Karol & Genowefa | 9, boy | Warsaw |
| 57. Stanislaw Wnuk | Antoni & Wimcentyna | 9, boy | Struzki |
| 58. Mieczyslaw Glica | Jan & Julianna | 8, boy | Struzki |
| 59. Jozef Spychala | Leon & Stanislawa | 7, boy | Struzki |
| 60. Marian Glica | Jan & Julianna | 6, boy | Struzki |
| 61. Czeslaw Spychala | Leon & Stanislawa | 5, boy | Struzki |
| 62. Tadeusz Wos | Wladyslaw & Marianna | 5, boy | Struzki |
| 63. Natalia B. Bobek | Wincenty & Stanislawa | 4, girl | Struzki |
| 64. Wieslawa Bobek | Wincenty & Stanislawa | 3, girl | Struzki |
| 65. Zofia Nowicka | Ignacy & Stanislawa | 2, girl | Struzki |
| 66. Jerzy Steborowski | Mieczyslaw & Honorata | 2, boy | Struzki |
| 67. Franciszka Glica | Daughter of Stanislawa | 1, girl | Struzki |

| | | | |
|---|---|---|---|
| 68. Tadeusz Nowicki | Ignacy & Stanislawa | 1, boy | Struzki |
| 69. Leon M. Tworek | Marian & Eleonora | 1, boy | Ossala |
| 70. Anna Wieruszewska | Jan & Regina | 1, girl | Ossala |
| 71. Teresa H. Bobek | Wincenty & Wladyslawa | 6 mos., girl | Struzki |
| 72. Mieczyslaw H. Wos | Son of Marianna | 5 mos., boy | Struzki |
| 73. Baby Drozdz | Ludwik & Stanislawa | 6 days, girl | Tursko-Zagumnie |
| 74. Wladyslawa Kurgan | Antoni & Marianna | 21, maiden | Luszyca |

## Chapter IV

# He Is Still Alive

Joe could hear light footsteps and then the shuffling of feet in the hallway. "Someone is coming, perhaps a stranger," thought the young and well-built man, and he hastily slipped under the mattress a copy of the underground newspaper. Soon the doorknob rattled, the door creaked open and into the room entered quickly a young woman with a beaming countenance.

"Do you know what, Joe?" she started.

"I know nothing," he answered.

"We are about to get a new apartment, dear Joe."

"What are you talking about? Where?" inquired Joe.

"Wait a moment. I'll explain everything to you. Just let me catch my breath."

After a short pause, the woman continued: "I was returning from Sulislawice with Frank Adamczak's wife, and she told me that they have a vacant apartment in their house in which his parents once lived. Since their death, no one has lived there. She told me that they would be glad to lease it. The apartment will certainly be better than the one which we have now."

"You are right, Mary! The Adamczaks' apartment will be much safer because it is near the forest. In case of necessity, we'll have a place to hide. It's too bad that we didn't know about it sooner."

"You would stay here all your life if it weren't for me," interrupted Mary.

"You are misjudging me, Mary. I am a very realistic and responsible man. Let me give you a kiss for bringing these good tidings." There was silence for a while. Mary, smiling, approached her husband, who kissed her affectionately.

"When shall we pack darling?" continued Joe.

"Right now," said Mary. "Mrs. Adamczak told me that

the apartment has been whitewashed and the floor has been scrubbed. What we have to do is start up the stove in order to warm up the place because it hasn't been heated all winter."

"Well, then, we must pack and that's it," decided Joe.

Mary took off her winter coat and, together with her husband, started to pack their belongings. By evening, everything was packed and stacked in the corner of the small living room.

In the morning, Joe and Mary moved to their new quarters. The apartment, although rather dark and filled with the odor of fresh lime, was large and comfortable. After several days, the tenants were settled in their new place. Their new quarters seemed to be ideal for peaceful living through the raging war and the terrible Nazi occupation.

It was the year 1943 and spring was slowly approaching. The sun was already higher in the sky and its warm rays were beginning to melt the snow. The people, tired and wary because of the long war, consoled each other with the saying: "As the sun is high, so Sikorski is nigh."*

The farmers who were preparing their implements for spring work in the fields thought to themselves and whispered to one another that in the coming fall they would not give the Germans their wheat. If they must give their grain, they hoped to give it to their own government.

On the country roads, the sleds were creaking and squeaking under the weight of the manure which they were carrying. The horses were snorting while pulling their heavy load to the dark spots in the fields where the snow had already partially disappeared.

Frank Adamczak, like most of the farmers in the village of Jeziory, was a very industrious and hard-working man. He and his family were on their feet early in the morning. While his wife prepared breakfast in the kitchen, he groomed his horses, fed them, and worked in the farmyard. Joe and Mary did not need an alarm clock to wake up in the morning. The early-rising Adamczaks were their most dependable clock. The noise made by the pots and pans in Mrs. Adamczak's kitchen and the loud pounding in the farmyard could awaken even a deaf person.

*General Wladyslaw Sikorski (1881-1943) was at that time Prime Minister of the Polish Government in exile in London and Commander-in-Chief of the Polish Legions that fought on the side of the Allies.

Soon the Adamczaks' new tenants coordinated their daily schedule with that of their landlords. They too began their day before sunrise and went to bed not too long after sunset. After a few weeks, they became accustomed to their new schedule and their life became orderly, harmonious, and peaceful. Joe and Mary liked their harmonious and peaceful life at the Adamczaks' farmhouse and hoped to stay there to the end of the war. However, the merciless fates had in store for them an unusual and cruel tragedy.

On that tragic day, February 7, 1943, the noise of Frank Adamczak's work in the farmyard awakened the young couple. Joe got up first in order to bring in some firewood from the shed. In the meantime, Mary placed the pots on the stove and began to build a fire. The kitchen was getting warmer and warmer every moment. The pleasant fire crackled in the wood-burning stove. The hissing steam was rising in curling white clouds from the pots. In a little while, breakfast was ready: boiled, mashed potatoes with bacon, borsch with cream, and fresh rye bread. Joe, kneeling beside the bed, was about to finish his morning prayers when Mary set the breakfast on the table.

"Sit down at the table, Joe, because the breakfast is getting cold and will not taste good."

"All right, Mary," replied Joe, getting up from his prayerful position.

The couple sat down to breakfast, said grace, and began to eat the steaming potatoes and warm white borsch. Before they finished breakfast, somebody knocked on their door.

"Come in," exclaimed Joe.

Into the room entered John*, wearing a fur hat. Although now a civilian, he still retained his military bearing as an officer.

"Good morning! How are you?" started John. "I am sorry for coming so early, but I am happy that you are already up. I could not sleep much last night; all sorts of thoughts were going through my mind and I am here to tell you about some of them."

"Please, tell us what you were thinking about, John,"

*John Mazgaj-Marglewski is Joe Mazgaj's first cousin. He was a public school teacher and an officer in the Polish Army before the Nazi invasion of Poland. John fought the Nazis during September of 1939. After World War II he became a dentist and had a very successful practice.

said Mary with a sincere curiosity.

After sitting comfortably at the table, John replied, "I thought about this long war and the situation in which we are forced to live. For too long we have been uprooted from our professional positions and forced to exist on the fringes of the farming community life. We are no longer farmers and are not fit to make a living as farmers or farmhands. We do not belong here, and everybody knows it. We belong in the urban communities we were forced out of by the Germans. Last night, when I thought about this ugly war, I came to the conclusion that the Germans are still too strong and therefore we cannot count on the end of the war coming this year. The war may last for a number of years. We cannot afford to sit and do nothing. We should not depend on the charity of our families who, after being robbed by the Germans, do not have much for themselves."

"But what are we able to do under the circumstances?" interrupted Joe.

"That's why I am here. I came to propose a partnership in business. We all know that in the cities, especially in Warsaw, there is a shortage of food, but in the villages the farmers can spare some bread and meat. The farmers have food but need clothing and shoes, which are available in the cities. Therefore, we will buy food in the villages and take it to Warsaw and bring back from there clothing, shoes, and other things which the farmers need. I think that by doing this we can help the people in need, make a little money, and the time will go faster for us. I know that you, Joe, would not make a good businessman, but Mary would be excellent at it."

"Do you know what, John? That's a great idea!" said Mary. "I had a similar idea some time ago but I was afraid to travel alone because it is dangerous for a woman."

"But what will happen when the police catch you, take your goods, and put you in prison?" asked Joe. "If you two intend to get involved in this type of business, you have to consider all the possibilities and be prepared for them."

"We will manage it somehow! Don't worry about it ahead of time, Joe. At least we can try," persuaded Mary.

"Yes, Joe. Mary is right!" said John.

"Well, then, you may try it, but I am warning you," concluded Joe.

Since John was not in a hurry to return home, Mary

prepared hot tea and put some pastry on the table. All three of them drank the tea, ate the pastry, and reminisced about the good life before the war. Their pleasant recollections made the time go fast.

It was about ten o'clock when the violent barking of the watch dog and the shouting brought them back to the reality of their present life.

"Take a look and see what's happening, Mary. Maybe someone is coming. Go look, my dear!" Joe asked of his wife. Mary went into the hallway and returned immediately with great haste. Her face was pale and she barely whispered, "Germans."

"What? Who?" questioned the men.

"I told you. Germans. They are trying to open the gate and their wagons are on the road in front of the gate," added Mary more audibly.

"We must run," said John as he approached the door. He walked out into the farmyard and headed for the firewood shed. There he disposed of his pistol and ammunition by throwing both of them into a large pile of firewood. As soon as the Germans managed to open the gate, they rushed toward the firewood shed and arrested John, as well as Frank Adamczak, who happened to be there also. The Germans led them to the front of the barn and ordered them to kneel and raise their hands.

In the meantime, Joe opened the window of their apartment and went through it into the orchard, which was on the eastern side of the farmhouse. So far, the Germans did not notice him, but when he began to dash toward the deep trench which was north of the house, the Germans saw him and shouted, "*Halt! Halt!*" Since Joe ignored the order and kept running, the Germans began to fire at him. He was already near the fence of the orchard, which was the last obstacle on his way to the trench. As he climbed the fence, the Germans kept firing at him, but they missed every time. As he ran between the fence and the trench, a German submachine gun opened up. At that point, Joe's instinct made him hit the ground. The Germans were convinced that their bullets hit Joe and began to approach him with their weapons ready to shoot. Joe pretended that he was dead. When they came close to Joe, they looked him over and one of them possibly an officer, said *"Das ist richtig."* (This is all right). Then they left Joe and returned to the farmyard to search the building.

When the Germans began to fire at Joe, Mrs. Adamczak took Mary into the larder and hid her under the floor. Soon the Germans were entering the house; their shouts and conversations were becoming progressively louder. Then Mary could hear the stamping of heavy military boots on the floor above her. She heard noises from the furniture being moved from place to place and the sobbing voice of Mrs. Adamczak.

"They're searching the house," thought Mary. "Soon they will be here, too. Joe must certainly have been killed. After all, they were shooting so much. If he is dead, then there is no reason for me to live either. Perhaps I should go out and give myself up and let them kill me."

At that point, the door to the larder creaked open. One German came in, followed by another. They were looking around and at the same time cursing: "Polish bandits." Mary was filled with fear and her heart was pounding like a hammer. She was afraid that the Germans in the larder might hear the pounding of her heart so she stopped breathing for a moment when they came close to where she was hiding and her heart stopped pounding. The instinct of self-preservation was at work. The Germans were searching everywhere and were removing various objects, but they did not look under the floor. Frustrated, they left the larder. The creaking door closed behind them. This was an obvious sign that the search of the larder was completed. Mary was saved.

After the Germans left Joe and went to search the farm buildings, he was convinced that he had an excellent opportunity to complete his run for the trench and thus save his life. Having surveyed the grounds around the farm building, he made a dash again toward the deep trench. One of the Germans noticed him, aimed his rifle and fired. The bullet pierced one of Joe's legs, but he kept running. The German fired again and Joe got hit in the second leg. He found himself in the trench, but he could not run anymore.

The German who wounded Joe in both legs followed him to the trench. He knew that his victim, who had fallen face-down on the bottom of the trench, was still alive, so he aimed his rifle again and fired into Joe's buttock. The bullet went between Joe's legs and ripped through his abdominal muscles and peritoneum. When the German came close to him, Joe pretended that he was expiring. The German was satisfied with his marksmanship and left Joe to die in the trench.

But Joe refused to die. The excruciating pain caused by the wounds in his legs and abdomen made him pass out from time to time, but the cold water from the melting snow, flowing like a little stream on the bottom of the trench, revived him again and again. Every time he lost consciousness, he felt that he was dying; every time he regained consciousness, he felt weaker and weaker. The open wounds in his legs and abdomen permitted his blood to flow quite freely. He noticed that the water around him in the trench was getting reddish. It seemed to him that he had been lying in the trench and dying for hours.

Suddenly he had a feeling that the Nazi gendarmes had left a long time ago and he could safely crawl out of the trench, stand up, and get some help. With one hand he grabbed at his abdomen, pushing in the intestines; with the other hand, he supported himself in an effort to get up. He managed to raise himself to his knees. Then he tried to get out of the trench. When he straightened himself up a little, the Germans, who were in their wagons and were ready to leave, noticed Joe. The one who had previously wounded Joe, Edward Vau, known to the area's population as "Bloody Eddy", jumped down from the wagon and went across the meadow toward Joe to complete the bloody work which he had previously failed to do.

"Come, do not be afraid. I will help you!" said the Nazi gendarme sneeringly. With his left hand, he grasped the wounded man and helped him to straighten up. Then, with his right hand, he withdrew his pistol from its holster, and saying, "Don't be afraid", he shot him in the back of the head. Joe stretched out his arms as though grasping for the air and fell backwards into the trench. The Nazi killer returned to his wagon and gave the order to drive on to the village of Ruszcza. As they left, they took John with them*. Joe was left in the trench, presumably dead.

As soon as the wagons with German gendarmes left for Ruszcza and disappeared behind the hill, Mary, who was practically out of her mind, rushed to Joe, who was lying motionless in a pool of water and blood. She put her hand on his chest. His

*John was taken by the Nazis to the Sandomierz Prison, interrogated and sent to the concentration camp in Auschwitz. He returned home after the Soviet and Polish soldiers liberated Auschwitz.

heart was beating.

"He still lives," she thought. "This is not the end; there is still hope. Perhaps the merciful Lord, through the intercession of Our Lady of Sulislawice, will save him," whispered Mary, shedding tears and trembling from her terrible experiences. Crying, she began to call out, "Please, someone, come and help me! Please help me to carry him out of this trench! He is still alive! Please come!"

Several frightened people who came out of their homes to see what had happened at the Adamczaks' farm responded to Mary's cries for help. They helped her pick Joe up by his arms and legs and carried him into the apartment. As they were carrying him, his blood was dripping along the way. Inside the apartment, they put him on the bed, gently removed his clothing, and washed away the mud and blood from his body. In order to stop the bleeding, Mary bound his wounds. In the meantime, one of the local farmers hitched his horses to the farm wagon and drove to Sulislawice to bring Father Jan Budzinski so he could give the last rites to Joe. At the same time, Stefan Padsiadly drove his wagon to Koprzywnica to bring a physician, Dr. George Ejmont.

Joe felt a little better after his wounds were dressed. The bleeding stopped and his consciousness stablized so he was able to answer his wife's questions. The people in Jeziory and Antonowka overcame their fear of the Germans and began to come to the Adamczaks' house to see what had happened. The first ones to arrive were Joe's parents and his sister Maria. His younger brother, Jan, happened to be in Polaniec at that time. His parents notified him of Joe's fate and he returned home two hours after the shooting. Soon the crowd of people increased considerably. The women who were present made necessary preparations for the coming of the priest with the Holy Viaticum.

Soon, Father Jan Budzinski, pastor of the Parish of Sulislawice, arrived in a carriage drawn by hard-driven and exhausted horses. When the people heard the tinkling of a small bell, they fell on their knees. The women, kneeling in two rows at the entrance of the house, began the popular eucharistic hymn: "At Thy Door I Stand, O Lord."

The priest descended from the carriage and immediately proceeded to the bed of the wounded man. The family left the bedroom. The door was closed. The confession began. After the confession was over, the priest opened the door so that the family and friends could enter the room and be present during the further ceremonies. After a short prayer, the priest took the Sacred Host, slightly elevated it, and said to the wounded man, "Receive, brother, the Holy Viaticum of the Body of Our Lord Jesus Christ", and placed it on his tongue. Then Father Budzinski administered to Joe the Sacrament of the Extreme Unction.

When the pastor concluded his priestly functions, he returned to the people and asked them to pray to God through the intercession of Our Lady of Sulislawice. He assured them that God would hear their prayers. As the priest was returning to the carriage, Joe's younger brother Jan returned from Polaniec and rushed to the wounded man's bedside. Joe was conscious and recognized Jan. When Jan asked him, "How are you feeling?", Joe responded, "The bone in my ankle hurts me so much." Jan checked his brother's ankle and noticed that it was slightly wounded by one of the German bullets.

After Father Budzinski left, everyone was filled with a new spirit. Practically everyone was convinced that Joe would survive. Mary was especially convinced of this. The words of the priest brought her peace, comfort, and confidence. "The Germans tried to kill him four times and he is still alive; there is something mysterious about it. Perhaps God does will that he not die yet...we should get him to the hospital as soon as possible," thought Mary.

Soon Stefan Padsiadly brought Dr. George Ejmont from Koprzywnica. The doctor rushed to Joe's bedroom, where he professionally dressed the wounded man's wounds and examined him. Then he asked Jan to follow him to the farmyard. "Your brother does not need more medical care," he said. "One hour from now he will be unable to speak any more and then the end will come unless there is a miracle through the intercession of Our Lady of Sulislawice." While concluding this statement, Dr. Ejmont pointed with his right hand toward Sulislawice.

The day came to a close and Joe was still alive and able to speak. Dr. Ejmont's prognosis did not materialize. Jan spent all night with his brother and Joe rested as well as possible under the conditions.

When morning came, Mary, Jan, and his friend, Waclaw Kos, decided to take Joe to the hospital in Tarnobrzeg. Soon the farm wagon was ready. Mary made a comfortable bed for her husband in the back of the wagon. She sat at Joe's feet and Jan and Waclaw sat in the driver's seat. The road to Tarnobrzeg was difficult and in some places very rough. The horses were driven at a slow pace to reduce Joe's pain to a minimum. Mary's parched lips whispered sincere prayers, asking God that Joe would arrive at the hospital alive. Her prayers were answered. Joe was still alive when they arrived at the front of the hospital in Tarnobrzeg.

While Mary and Waclaw Kos remained in the wagon, Jan entered the hospital and began to look for the chief surgeon. Soon he found Dr. Rusinowski and asked him to examine Joe and admit him to the hospital. Dr. Rusinowski decided to examine the patient in the wagon. After he removed the dressing placed on the wounds by Dr. Ejmont, he looked at Mary, Jan, and Waclaw and said, "Why did you bring this corpse to me? Neither I nor anybody else can save his life." What a statement to make in front of a patient! What kind of bedside manner was this for a physician who had taken the Hippocratic Oath to save human lives? Needless to say, all of them were shocked. Nevertheless, Jan began to plead with Dr. Rusinowski. He said, "Sir, my brother is alive and conscious; please admit him to the hospital and operate on him."

"I have no place for him in the hospital," replied Dr. Rusinowski with arrogance.

"If you cannot admit him to the hospital, won't you dress his wounds, Doctor?" asked Jan.

"I have no bandages to dress his wounds!" replied the angry surgeon.

"My brother's wounds were dressed when we brought him to you. You took his bandages off during the examination. Please replace them. You must do it; this is your duty!" argued Jan. The surgeon gave in and dressed Joe's wounds. He then walked away without a word.

In spite of the scandalous behavior of Dr. Rusinowski, which was very painful and discouraging to Mary, Jan, and Waclaw, they did not give up hope of saving Joe's life. They decided to travel to the Holy Ghost Hospital in Sandomierz. The road from Tarnobrzeg to Sandomierz was rather good and easy to travel so they reached Sandomierz in the afternoon. As soon as they arrived at the hospital, Mary met one of the Sister of

Charity who worked there and asked her whether she could speak to Dr. Alexsander Dobkiewicz. The sister found Dr. Dobkiewicz and brought him to Mary, who explained her husband's condition to the surgeon. Dr. Dobkiewicz ordered her to bring Joe to the examination room. After examining Joe, he said to Mary and Jan, "I will do my best which is humanly possible and I will leave the rest to the Almighty God."

Soon Joe was in the surgery room. Dr. Dobkiewicz, an excellent surgeon who valued human life very highly, began the surgery. First he sutured the large abdominal wound. Then he treated both wounds on Joe's legs. Finally, he undertook the most difficult part of the operation; that is, the removal of the pistol bullet which entered the back of the head below the brain and lodged itself under the left eye. Dr. Dobkiewicz made the incision near Joe's left eye and removed the bullet. "Thank God!" exclaimed the surgeon. The operation was a success. However, Joe had to remain in the hospital for a long time.

His wife, happy with the successful outcome of the operation, rented a room in town in order to visit Joe every day and cater to his needs. A few days after the operation there was a marked improvement in the health of the patient, even though the pistol bullet destroyed Joe's optic nerve, thus depriving him of sight in the left eye. The gloomy days full of pain and anxiety were replaced with the bright rays of life, which inevitably would still at times be darkened by some stormy clouds.

During his extended hospitalization, Joe had many visitors who came to cheer him up and assure him of their prayers. Mary was by his side day in and day out. His parents and relatives visited him as much as possible. Jan, his brother, visited rather frequently.

After five weeks of hospitalization, Joe was recovering well and gaining strength. He was looking forward to the day he would be discharged from the hospital and would be able to return to a normal life.

On March 19, the day the church celebrates the Feast of St. Joseph and the day on which Joe always celebrated his Name's Day, his younger brother Jan came to visit him and wish him Happy Name's Day. He spent a couple of hours with Joe and left the hospital shortly before noon. At about noontime, a couple of uninvited visitors, members of the Nazi Gendarmerie, entered the hospital hall in which Joe and a number of other patients were. They were looking for a Polish policeman who while in the service of the Germans was attacked and wounded by somebody and brought to the hospital for treatment. The wounded policeman happened to be in the hall with Joe.

Joe recognized one of the uninvited visitors as the killer "Bloody Eddy" and began to pray that the Nazi killer would not recognize him. Soon the gendarmes found the wounded policeman and interrogated him about the circumstances under which he was attacked and wounded. They wanted to find out who the attacker was.

When they completed the questioning of the wounded policeman and were on their way to the door of the hall, "Bloody Eddy" seemed to recognize Joe. As both of the Nazis approached Joe' s bed, he became aware that they were under the influence of alcohol. They transfixed Joe with their drunken eyes, eager to find out who he was. "Bloody Eddy" appeared to be pensive, trying to recollect something. He peered into the patient's face with a great intensity and seemed to think, "Where have I seen this man before?" He pondered for a while and all of a sudden he recognized Joe. Extremely surprised, he asked, "Is that you? Are you still alive?" Turning to his companion, he said, "I shot him four times and he is still alive! That's impossible and incredible! Now I'll finish him for sure." As he was saying this, "Bloody Eddy" began to pull out his pistol. But his companion grabbed the killer's hand and said, *"Du hast viel zeit"* (You have a lot of time), pulling him away toward the door.

As soon as the gendarmes left the hospital, there was a great degree of commotion there. The sisters notified Dr. Dobkiewicz about Joe's predicament and he, in turn, notified the local post of the Home Army. The members of the post came immediately, removed Joe from the hospital hall to a bathroom, helped him to put on his street clothing, and took him to a horse-drawn cab which waited in front of the hospital. By 2:00 p.m., Joe was gone and no one in the hospital knew where he had gone.

At about 6:00 p.m., "Bloody Eddy" came to the hospital to kill Joe but did not find him in his bed. He was extremely disappointed and angry. He asked Dr. Dobkiewicz what had happened to his patient. The surgeon explained that according to the report he received from the nurses on the floor, Joe had left the hospital. He added that he, as a physician, treated equally all the patients who came to him and did not inquire into their background. "Bloody Eddy" accepted the surgeon's explanation as valid and did not cause him any problems.

The members of the Home Army placed Joe in one of their safe houses and then took him to another place and then still another, where he recuperated under the watchful supervision of capable physicians and his wife. When Joe was well enough to travel by farm wagon, the post of the Home Army in Sandomierz sent a messenger to Jan so he could come with a farm wagon and take his brother away. On the same day, Jan went to Sandomierz and picked up Joe and Mary, who were staying with a family in a secluded home. From Sandomierz, the three of them rode the farm wagon through the countryside to the village of Wiazownica, where their aunt Stepien and her family lived. There, Joe was to spend the time of his convalescence.

The village of Wiazownica was situated in the immediate vicinity of a large forest known to the local population as the Forest of Staszow. In spite of the fact that Wiazownica was away from heavily traveled roads, it was nevertheless necessary to take all precautions so the Nazis would not discover Joe was there. No strangers were allowed to enter his bedroom. Joe and Mary had to give up their correspondence with relatives and friends. With the exception of parents, his brother Jan, and sister Maria, relatives were discouraged from visiting Joe. The neighbors who knew about Joe's presence in the home were warned to be confidential. The aunt's children, Bogdan and Frank, were asked not to talk about Joe to anybody.

Now Joe was spending his entire days talking with his wife, his aunt, and his nephews. When Mary was preparing meals and he was alone, Joe thought about his past life.

The years of his childhood appeared to him as in reality: he thought about his playmates and the tender love of his mother and grandmother. Then came to his mind the years of his boyhood and grade school in Sulislawice. There were so many moments of joy and happiness. His friends always respected him because he was a good student and because of his physical strength, which he developed by helping his father in the blacksmith shop.

Then Joe transferred his thoughts to the technical school in Wloclawek. His classmates and his sweethearts--what had happened to them? Were they still alive or dead? Then be began to recollect his experiences in the Polish Navy in Pinsk and later in Gdynia. His new friends and his new life in the navy had many attractions and brought him much joy. Everything in his new life was so interesting and new. At that time, he was full of energy and life. And today, what? Lying confined to his bed, weak and exhausted. When the service in the navy ended, then came the Military Technical School in Warsaw. Constant assignments and studies did not leave much time for other activities. Time was passing very quickly. It was at that busy period of his life that he met Mary. Her charm irresistibly attracted and delighted him. She was always so good and pleasant...

All of a sudden, his bedroom door opened and Mary entered the room, bringing the patient his dinner.

"Aren't you sleeping, Joe?" she asked.

"No, Mary. I've just been lying here and thinking."

"And what were you thinking about, my dear?"

"At this moment, about you, Mary. Do you remember our first meeting?"

"I remember very well. Never did I think at that time that you would be my husband. But you had better eat, Joe, because the soup will cool off. When you have eaten, we will then talk about the old times."

"I am eating already, Mary, my precious one. Oh, how delicious this soup is! This reminds me of my mother's cooking at home."

Mary smiled and with a great deal of satisfaction accepted the praises of her husband. After all, she was a woman, and naturally there is no praise that can please any woman more than that of her beauty and her ability to cook.

"Now see, Mary, I have eaten it all," continued Joe.

"I will now bring you some tea. So wait a while and don't fall off to sleep," said Mary, leaving the room with the empty plate. The tea Mary brought was very hot, and when Joe had finished drinking it, he wiped the perspiration from his forehead. Through the slightly open window could be heard the chirping of the birds and the voices of playing children, and a pleasing fragrance from the pine trees growing around the house could be detected.

"What else were you thinking about, Joe?" asked Mary, picking up the topic of their interrupted conversation.

"I was thinking about my childhood and my younger days. I have such pleasant memories of those days. Do you remember, Mary, how happy we were in Rembertow? That was our first home. Do you remember the large rooms and the lattice window? We lacked nothing except perhaps the proverbial bird's milk. Only once did I feel bad there."

"When was that? And why, Joe?" interrupted Mary.

"I never told you about it because I did not want to alarm you, dear. I don't know why it entered my head today. It happened in the very beginning of our stay in Rembertow. It was night. Quiet as usual. I was awakened by what seemed to be the muffled scratching of a cat on our bedroom window. Without arousing you, I got up quietly and, going on tiptoes along the wall, approached the window. The scratching on the window did not cease. At first I could not tell what it was because I was too sleepy. Then I noticed the movement of a thin piece of wire which someone was using in an attempt to open the latch on our window. Certainly it must be a thief or even a bandit, I thought. I had nothing at hand with which to protect myself or to frighten away the malefactor. Suddenly, I remembered that only the day before I had been using a hammer and had not yet taken it back to the toolshed. It was lying in the corner of the bedroom. Noiselessly, I went to the place where the hammer was lying. It was in the same spot where I had left it. I took it in my hand and again approached the window. The manipulation with the latch was still continuing and I could not understand why it would not open. I had already thought out my plan of action: when the criminal opened the window and started to enter the room, I would strike him in the head with the hammer and then call the police.

"While I was standing there waiting for the housebreaker to start entering the house, I suddenly became aware of the fact that the realization of my plan would be the same as homicide. Regardless of who he might be, he was still a human being and maybe even a very poor fellow. He might even have a wife and children. I felt sorry for him. I coughed loudly and then approached the light switch and turned on the lights in the room. The manipulations at the window stopped immediately and then I heard a sound on the street of someone hastily running away. I turned off the light and returned to bed. The next day I fixed the latch on the window so that it could not be opened with any kind of wire. For the next several nights I was on guard, but the attempt to open the window was not repeated."

"And you didn't tell me anything about it, Joe! This is the first time I hear of it!" interrupted Mary, deep in thought and listening intently to the narration of her husband.

"I did not want to tell you anything about it so you would not be afraid to live there, and so you could sleep peacefully. Today that is history, and therefore you can know all about it. But imagine, Mary," continued Joe, "how this event of many years past, about which I just told you, is associated with my recent experience. I have the odd feeling that if I had killed that person, I would have been destroyed by the German's bullets. Now I am only wounded. And maybe I am wounded because as a young boy, in a fit of anger, I wounded a man who happened to be my uncle and godfather. I know now that I committed an evil act. I was very young at the time and I forgot myself. I understand now the moral of Prus's novel, *The Returning Wave.*"

"You'd better not talk about that, Joe, because it's tiring you. Just lie down and try to sleep while I wash the dinner dishes and clean up the kitchen."

"All right, Mary, you go about your work and I will try to sleep," said Joe, closing the conversation.

Mary stepped out of the room and quietly closed the door behind her. Joe tried to sleep but was unsuccessful. His thoughts again started to return to events of the past. September 1, 1939, Nazi Germany attacks Poland; the first German aerial attacks on Warsaw; mobilization and then the constant march to the East; a shortage of food and water; short periods of rest at night on the cold ground under the wagons; and later the traitorous attack by the Soviets on the brave Polish Army, defending itself against the Germans; battles with the Soviets, captivity, and then the successful escape; later, the long, hard march by side roads toward home, to Rembertow; and finally, the packing of their belongings and the journey to the parental home in Jeziory; the stay there and later the misunderstanding between Mary and his mother; moving into the dark room rented from the Stawiarz family; and then moving into the Adamczaks' place and the tragic happenings of the last weeks. With these recollections, Joe fell asleep, but his mind continued to work even subconsciously.

He dreamed that he saw "Bloody Eddy" dressed in a

hospital gown stained with big spots of blood, human blood. In some places the blood was already dry; in other places it was fresh and soaking into the fabric. There were so many bloodstains that it was difficult to tell what color the gown was, white or red. It could be taken for a red gown because the fresh blood which was soaking into the fabric was constantly enlarging the existing stains and the white of the hospital gown had been displaced with the red of the blood. There was already practically no white to be seen. The blood was everywhere, even on the hands and face of the Nazi policeman. The bloodstains on his face made him appear even more terrible.

In his blood-smeared hands "Bloody Eddy" was holding a long butcher knife, its pointed edge directed toward the throat of Joe, who was lying on the ground. Along the sharp edge of the knife there was dark red blood, dripping in large drops from its sharp point. The bloodthirsty policeman was coming closer and closer to his victim. Joe wanted to defend himself but was unable to do so because it seemed as though his extremities had changed into heavy weights of lead. He was, therefore, undergoing horrible suffering. The murderer dept coming closer and closer and was already placing the pointed edge of the knife to Joe's throat. Joe felt the moisture of the drops of blood from the knife and, simultaneously, the slight-but-penetrating pricking of the knife. He wanted to scream for help but could not do so. Something was choking him and silencing his voice. He was moving his tongue and his lips but was giving out no sounds.

"Bloody Eddy" was laughing sarcastically at his helpless victim and then driving the knife further into his throat, saying, "You were a bandit. You wanted a free Poland. Now you will be destroyed. You will die like a dog!"

The sharp point of the knife slowly penetrated through Joe's throat, but strange as it may seem, the pain seemed to subside. Joe tried once again to shout, and this time his sonorous-but-terrified voice resounded throughout the whole house.

"It is you who are the bandit," cried out Joe with all his might. "You murder the innocent. You are the criminal and the bandit because you are killing me!"

Suddenly, Joe opened his eyes. He awakened. At his bedside stood Mary, frightened.

"What's wrong with you, Joe? What happened? Why are you screaming?" she asked.

"It's nothing, Mary. I had a nightmare. I was dreaming that "Bloody Eddy" was killing me the fifth time. If you only knew how terrible he looked. He had a monstrous face and his hands were smeared with human blood!" said Joe, feeling his neck with his hands and trying to move his feet.

His neck was whole and his feet could be moved, although with a slight sensation of pain because of his wounded legs and abdomen.

"Yes, it was only a dream," continued Joe, "but it frightened me because it seemed so real."

"I, too, was frightened because I thought that somebody actually broke into your room through the window and wanted to murder you. But when I opened the door and saw you in bed, I realized that it must have been only a dream."

"What can such a dream mean?" asked Joe, becoming a bit calmer after his terrifying experience.

"I did not study Freudian psychology, so I do not know much about interpretation of dreams," replied Mary.

"Of course we do read in Holy Scripture that God permitted certain people to have prophetic dreams, but those are exceptions and happen only in very important moments in the history of humanity. Don't give another thought to this "Bloody Eddy" and you won't be bothered with such dreams anymore," said Mary.

The conversation of the husband and wife on dreams was interrupted by the dialogue of two women outside near the house.

Mary glanced out the window. By the fence stood the aunt with a bundle of weeds on her back. She was conversing with a neighbor on the other side of the fence. Although Mary could not see the woman on the other side of the fence, her voice could be heard very clearly through the slightly open window.

"How are, my friend?" inquired the aunt.

"Fine, thank you. And how are you?"

"Fine, also," answered the aunt.

"How is your work coming along?"

"Oh, I have a lot of work," complained the aunt.

"This year everybody has a lot of work because of the frequent rains and heavy growth of weeds out in the fields. And everything waits to be done by us. If we could only see some results from our work. Plant, weed, hoe, harvest, and then when everything is ready, the authorities send you an order to turn everything over to those Germans. They don't even ask you if you would like to retain something at least for the children. No consideration. Only give, give, give, and that's it."

"No truer words were said, my friend! But what can we do? Our only hope is God. If our merciful Lord does not save us from these Germans, no one else will!" cried out the aunt confidently.

"But do you know what? I almost forgot to tell you," the woman on the other side of the fence interrupted in a low voice.

"What?" asked the aunt excitedly, with typical feminine curiosity.

"The Cossacks were in the village yesterday," said the woman hurriedly, as though anxious to share this news with someone.

"The Cossacks were? Are you sure? Who told you so?" asked the aunt.

"My husband was hoeing the potatoes yesterday and I was helping him lead the horse--it's just a young horse and that was his first day out in the fields. We passed over one section of the field several times and then we noticed Stan Czajka's wife coming toward us. She said that the Cossacks were in their yard. I asked her what they wanted and she said that they asked for hay and oats for their horses. I asked her how they were able to converse with each other and she said that their language is similar to ours and she was able to understand them. When I asked her if Stan gave them the hay, she replied that her husband isn't so foolish as to give anything to just anyone who asks for it. He told them not to ask for anything but to run away from there as fast as they could because if the partisans caught them, they would regret it. When the Cossacks heard that, they straightened their caps, got up on their wagons, struck the horses with their whips, and were gone. They kept turning around to see if someone was chasing them.

"I thought to myself at the time that Stan Czajka acted foolishly. He shouldn't have mentioned the partisans because that may bring misfortune to the village. Yesterday the Cossacks fled because there were only four of them, but they won't forget what happened! Next time there will come about a hundred of them, and then not even the partisans will be able to control them. They may burn down the entire village, as has happened in many places. After all, they do what the Germans tell them to do. If they tell them to burn the village, they will burn it; if they tell them to shoot down all the inhabitants, they will shoot everyone. My husband says we'll have to wait and see what happens. It's the will of God. We will see what will come about from all this. Sometimes from a big cloud only a small rain falls. In any event, though, we must be vigilant. And in case anything happens, we must run and hide. As though we don't have enough troubles, we have to have this to think about."

"That's true. That's true. It seems that misfortune always follows us. No one knows what will happen next."

So saying, the aunt glanced in the direction of the window to Joe's bedroom. It appeared that she was getting ready to leave because she lifted the bundle of weeds which had been leaning against the trunk of a tree. It was obvious that it was important to her to share her knowledge with those in the house.

"I must go now because the pigs are squealing in the pen. I have to fix them their feed. Thank you for the news," concluded the aunt.

"Oh, you're welcome," replied the woman on the other side, and they both parted.

Joe as well as Mary heard the entire conversation through the slightly open window and their faces were becoming gloomier as time went on. When the women parted, Mary was the first one to start the conversation.

"You see, Joe, what has happened. What are we to do now?"

"Don't worry, Mary, everything will be all right," said Joe, trying to comfort his wife although he himself was somewhat disturbed by the situation.

"We will have to think of something," said Mary. "But let's wait until our aunt gets here; she may be able to advise us."

After a little while, the aunt entered the room. By the expression on her face, one could see that she was both excited and worried.

"Do you know what has happened?" she asked, and without waiting for an answer she started to tell from the beginning what she had learned from her neighbor. Mary interrupted her and informed her that she and Joe had heard practically the entire conversation between the aunt and the neighbor. The aunt was disappointed that she could not complete her story with all of its details.

They immediately took up the problem at hand; namely, what to do with Joe in case of an attack on the village by the Cossacks. Mary offered her idea of transporting her husband to the forest and waiting there until the danger passed. The aunt, on the other hand, was opposed to this plan because she feared that in the forest he would be faced with greater danger. She suggested, instead, transporting Joe to the fields, the place of daily labor.

"He can lie on the wagon the same as in the bed," said the aunt. "And, besides, it will be better for his health to be out in the fresh air."

Joe preferred the suggestion of the aunt rather than his wife's idea and decided, for the duration of the danger, to ride out every morning to the fields.

Early the next morning, the aunt's house was a place of great activity. The aunt was hurriedly preparing breakfast and noisily moving the pots in the fireplace. Mary was arranging the bedding and pillows on the wagon, which was brought around to the doorway. The aunt's eldest son, Bogdan, was feeding the horses and brushing them with a currycomb. Before Mary could finish arranging the bedding on the wagon, the aunt was calling everyone to breakfast. After breakfast, the women wrapped the patient in a blanket, and with the help of Bogdan and the younger son, Frank, they carried him onto the wagon, appropriately prepared by Mary. Bogdan hitched the horses to the wagon and after the women seated themselves in the wagon, the aunt told her son to start rolling and instructed her other son, Frank, to guard the house and possessions.

After the death of her husband, the aunt managed the affairs of the household herself, and her sons, who were quite obedient, were a great help to her. Whatever she requested them to do, they did without any words or questions. Consequently, the household did not fall apart after the death of its head but maintained the same high standard.

The wagon left the yard and came onto the road in the field which belonged to the aunt and which stretched as far as the limits of the fields. The wheels of the wagon rolled silently over the sandy road. The sky was progressively becoming lighter. In the eastern part of the sky could be seen a red glare, as though from a tremendous fire, which with every minute became stronger until finally there appeared the rising sun. It seemed as though the early-morning rays of the sun frightened the whitish fog rising slowly over the fields but now starting to fall swiftly to the ground and moistening even more the wheat which was already wet from the life-giving dew. The larks were flying around and sending forth in interrupted sounds their morning song of spring.

From his high position in the wagon, Joe was looking around in all directions and seemed to be bewitched with and amazed at what he saw. He called to the women and Bogdan, "Look, how marvelous all this is! How tall the wheat is, and the grass. When did all this grow? Wonders everywhere."

"This year we have a fine and warm spring, so everything is growing very well. And the older folks are saying that the harvests will be plentiful," replied the aunt.

"That is possible," added Mary enthusiastically.

"Do you know what?" continued Joe. "In the spring, it seems that man finds even a human life more beautiful and more valuable."

"Yes, that's true, Joe. In the spring, life seems to be most beautiful and most treasured. But I think that man appreciates the beauty of life the most when the time comes for him to part with this world," philosophized Mary.

"Yes, Mary. There is so much truth in what you have said. I have experienced that myself. When it seemed to me that the hours of my life were numbered, I wanted so much then to live. I wanted to live at least to see the end of the war, to see the downfall of the Germans, to see Poland rise again free. Therefore, I am grateful to God that, despite everything, I still live, and that I am able today to look at this world and the indescribable beauty of nature with which God clothed this world," continued Joe in a tired voice.

The horses stopped. They had arrived at the place of work. Bogdan was the first to jump down from the wagon. He threw to the horses a bundle of hay which had already been prepared at home before departure. Then the women stepped down from the wagon. The aunt, together with Bogdan, went off to start weeding the millet. Mary remained for a while longer with Joe, inquiring as to his comfort and his needs. Joe insisted that he was all right and that he needed nothing. All he wanted was to take in slowly all the beauties of nature around him.

There was nothing else for Mary to do but to go after the others to the section of the field where the millet was growing and help them.

"I will come back after a while, Joe, in case you might need anything," said Mary, leaving the wagon.

"Very well, Mary, come back later," agreed Joe, watching his wife as she went off into the fields.

Before Mary reached the place where the aunt and Bogdan were working, she could hear from the direction of Bukowa at first a single shot and then a series of shots. At the sound of the shots, Mary immediately returned to the wagon. She was followed by the aunt and then by Bogdan, who immediately started to ready the horses for departure. They discussed and considered what to do. Bogdan wanted to flee with the wounded man, but he did not know where to go. The aunt advised not to move from the place but to wait to see what would happen.

"Should the Germans or even the Cossacks come here," she reasoned, "they won't be surprised to find a wagon standing out in the field and people working nearby. On the other hand, if they should see someone running away in the wagon, they will either chase after it or shoot at the driver."

The shooting did not stop and even at times seemed to be increasing. Bullets were whistling in the air. The horses were becoming excited and were pricking up their ears.

"It's too bad that we didn't take Frank along with us; in the village, he may be in actual danger," said the aunt.

"Don't worry, Mother," said Bogdan. "Frank is tending the cows in the pasture. When he sees the Cossacks entering the village, he will run into the fields."

"That's right, Auntie. You don't have to be afraid about Frank because he is very clever and will manage. But I'm afraid that the entire village is threatened with some great danger," added Mary.

"It may not be so bad though, because if the partisans are shooting that means they feel strong enough to defend themselves. If they felt outnumbered, they would sit back quietly," said Bogdan, who had collected himself and was feeling more sure of himself now." What would you know about it?" scolded his mother. "There are only a few partisans, and they don't have the kind of weapons that the Germans and the Cossacks have, so they won't be able to defend themselves for long."

"Well, you will see, Mother, if it doesn't happen the way I say," cut in Bogdan.

"Don't talk so much. Instead, come and we'll take up our work again. We all can't stand here by the wagon or we'll betray the wounded one," said the aunt, ending the discussion.

So all three went back to their interrupted work. Every so often, Mary would glance all around the fields to see if by any chance the Cossacks or the Germans were appraoching.

Joe lay in the wagon and prayed. He was calm; perhaps the calmest of them all because he had the conviction within himself that, at the moment, death had no claim on him. It could be that his miraculous escape from sure death enhanced this feeling of confidence in God's protection. Every once in a while he would hear the hurrying footsteps of people, which meant that the people were fleeing from that section of the village nearest the place of battle. The women tried to question those running away to learn some details, but they, in their hurry, limited their answers only to the words "Germans" or "Cossacks".

Around ten o'clock in the forenoon, the shooting ceased entirely and the more forward villagers cautiously approached the village seeking some information. At noon, Bogdan noticed a wagon leaving the village. He pointed it out to his mother and Mary. The mother sent him to the man in the wagon to find out about the situation in the village. Bogdan went willingly and with a great deal of curiosity. In a little while, he returned with news, and from a distance exclaimed triumphantly:

"My words have come true. Didn't I tell you, Mother, that the partisans would chase out the Cossacks? Tony Czajka says that the Cossacks were escaping with such haste that they were losing their boots and caps along the way."

"How was it, Bogdan?" interrupted Mary.

"Czajka says that the Cossacks came from the direction of Bukowa. There were about twenty-five wagons and several Cossacks in each wagon. Probably there were some Germans. The partisans, as usual, had their guard stationed at the crossroads, where the old cross stands. Tony says there were two guards. One guard belonged to the partisans of the Home Army (A.K.) headquartered in the homes near the forest, and the second guard belonged to the Peasants' Battalions (B.Ch.) which several days ago came into our territory. One group placed its machine guns on one side of the road; the other group, on the opposite side.

"When the partisans noticed the Cossacks approaching, they didn't interfere with them at first. But as soon as the Cossacks reached the small wooded area, the partisans opened fire. Apparently, the Cossacks became panicky and didn't know what to do because they didn't expect such heavy firing from the partisans. The horses became frightened and broke the shafts of the harness. Probably there remain many broken wagons and killed horses along the road. Some of the Cosssacks left their horses and wagons and fled into the forest. Others turned on the spot and fled in the direction from which they came."

"Thanks be to God that everything has ended so well. God grant that these robbers will not return!" the aunt added to Bogdan's report.

"Perhaps we should eat something now," suggested Bogdan.

"Good idea, Bogdan. Get the food from the basket and we will eat because it is already past the noon hour," agreed the aunt.

When Bogdan brought the food, the conversation ceased for a while. Joe ate slowly because he was asking Bogdan questions about the details of the battle. Joe was happy on account of the partisans' victory.

The afternoon passed quickly and quietly. In the evening, everyone returned home to spend a peaceful night since the Germans had stopped coming into the area at night except perhaps in great numbers. At home, everything was in order and Frank was waiting at the gate for those returning from the fields.

The next day, Joe was again taken to the field. This continued for several days. When the danger had passed, Joe again lay in bed and, through the open window, looked out on the beautiful green trees and listened to the chirping of the birds, or spent his time in conversation with his wife. Each day he felt stronger and promised that shortly he would be able to get up and walk by himself. His wounds were healing very well now and he was regaining his good humor; the sound of his laughter could be heard throughout the whole house.

Several days later, Joe did get up from his bed, with great difficulty. He had to learn to walk again--like a child. Mary usually supported him in his walks around the room; when she was absent, a chair served as his support. His appetite and sleep returned to normal. Joe slept now like a baby; nightmares did not bother him anymore. Life in the aunt's house was peaceful again.

One evening, however, there appeared two young men armed with rifles and grenades. On their caps was the Polish White Eagle. They introduced themselves as partisans in the Home Army (A.K.) and politely but firmly demanded that Bogdan hitch up the horses to the wagon and go with them. They assured him that there was nothing to fear, that he and the horses would be home by morning. It was not necessary to repeat this demand to Bogdan. He called Frank to help him and immediately the horses were hitched up to the wagon. For some time, he had dreamed of something like this happening. After a while, everything was ready for the journey. The partisans expressed their gratitude for the horses and bidding everyone good night seated themselves on the wagon. Bogdan's mother brought out to him his cap and coat because the nights were sometimes cool.

When they got out on the road, Bogdan noticed that in many farmyards farmers were hitching up their horses to their wagons and the partisans were helping them. Soon there was a long line of wagons on the road, heading east. People, coming out of their houses, stood by the roadside, peered at the passersby, and wished them a safe return. The partisans thanked them for their good wishes and waved goodbye. When the partisans came to the outskirts of the village, they took the road that turned into the wooded area. After a little while, the caravan disappeared into the black forest. The surprised riders were told to place their wagons and horses in a row so that at any moment they could respond to further orders. More partisans came to the wagons and forbade the drivers to smoke or to converse loudly. The drivers were excited and very curious as to what they would be transporting and when they would begin their work. They tried to learn something about it from the partisans but not one would discuss the subject. One of the partisans explained that shortly they would know what they were to do.

The hours were passing one by one; midnight was approaching and nothing was happening. From time to time one could hear only that small groups of partisans were moving here and there in the darkness of the night. This added even more mystery and increased the curiosity of the drivers. Bogdan was moving about impatiently by his wagon because his curiosity would not permit him to stand still. He was looking constantly into the darkness surrounding him but he could see nothing. Soon after midnight, a small group of partisans arrived and the chief of the group told the drivers to be ready because in a little while their services would be needed. The drivers, therefore, adjusted the horses' harnesses and waited for the eventual signal. The first hour after midnight was approaching and the moon appeared in the sky, slightly illuminating the darkness of the night.

From the northwestern direction could be heard the distant sound of an airplane. With every moment the sound became more pronounced, and finally it was heard above the heads of the partisans and drivers. The airplane flew over the forest and then descended to a lower altitude and began to give some light signals. At the same moment, on the fields between the village and the forest, there flashed on a great number of various-colored flashlights, held by persons standing in prearranged positions so that the light formed some definite pattern. Evidently the pilot noticed this signal because the airplane tilted slightly on its left wing, circled around, and retraced its former route. This time he did not give any light signals but lowered himself even more. Suddenly a noise was heard from the direction of the airplane and then many large parachutes opened up in the air and dropped to the ground.

Now the mystery was solved. The drivers knew exactly why they had been brought here. They were happy that in a little while they would be able to see with their own eyes that which was dropping from the airplane. They were proud that their horses and wagons were chosen to transport the weapons needed in the struggle for the liberation of their country. Bogdan seemed to be the happiest one there; he could hardly wait for the moment of departure. The airplane returned once more and again dropped a cloud of parachutes. Then, as a farewell signal, the pilot truned on and off the lights on the wings of the plane and flew away.

Now the feverish task started. The drivers and the partisans went out to gather the weapons and other equipment and load them onto the wagons. Despite the fact that the wheat was already tall, it was not too difficult to find the containers because the colorful parachutes indicated where they were lying.

Also, attached to the containers and crates were phosphorescent plates which shone in the dark, thereby disclosing their location even from a distance. The partisans were loading these packages onto wagons which were being slowly driven along the roads in the fields. The drivers were helping them in this work and were surprised that the containers were so heavy.

When everything had been loaded onto the wagons, the chief of the partisan group went from wagon to wagon and checked the contents. Obviously, everything was in order, because the command was given to depart. The horses started pulling their heavily-laden wagons. When they were on the sandy road, the partisans had to help the horses by pushing the wagons. The column of wagons, protected from all sides, moved slowly in the direction of the Forest of Gorki. After an hour's ride, the wagons entered the forest and came to a stop. The chief of the partisans group called together all of the drivers and informed that they would now turn over their horses and wagons to the partisans and wait there for their return.

It was almost daybreak when the horses and empty wagons were returned to the place where the drivers were waiting. The horses were wet from sweat and very tired. Hurriedly, each driver got into his wagon to return home before daybreak. Before departing, the partisans thanked the drivers for their help and warned them to keep secret all that they had seen.

Bogdan lashed the horses with his whip and departed for home. He was satisfied because this night he understood many things which had previously puzzled him. Never did he think that the partisans had so much strength. Neither did he know that the Home Army (A.K.) was obtaining weapons and war materiel from the West. He was surprised that the partisans were so splendidly organized and trained. As he approached the village, he wondered if those at home had seen what happened that night on the field between the village and the forest.

"Surely they must have been sleeping as usual and don't know a thing about it," thought Bogdan, rubbing with his fist his eyes, which were closing on him because he was so sleepy. "Surely they don't know anything," he repeated to himself in a low voice.

In the meantime, at home, no one was sleeping. Joe did fall asleep after Bogdan's departure and Mary followed his example. The aunt, however, could not sleep because she was constantly wondering what was happening to her son. She tried to sleep but was unable to do so. So she walked up and down in her room and listened for the sound of the returning wagon. On the outside, silence reigned.

The aunt knelt before the picture of Our Lady of Sulislawice and began reciting the rosary for the repose of the soul of her husband. She was finishing the third mystery of the rosary when she heard the sound of a low-flying airplane. She approached the window and observed that the airplane turned on and then turned off the lights on its wings.

"That means something," thought the woman.

Curious, she went out into the garden in order to get a better view of this phenomenon. First she saw the plane circling around in the air, and then she observed the parachutes dropping toward the ground. She ran as fast as she could into the bedroom of Joe and Mary and awakened them.

"Look! Something is happening, because an airplane is flying over the fields, flashing on and off its red lights and throwing down something attached to parachutes!" shouted the aunt feverishly. Mary immediately jumped up out of bed and ran outside. Joe dragged himself out of bed also, and supporting himself against the wall, came out slowly into the garden. Frank opened the doors to the barn, where he usually slept during the summer, and rubbing his sleepy eyes looked up into the sky. The airplane was once again releasing its load. The parachutes were opening up with a slight cracking noise and slowly floating toward the ground.

"They are dropping, on parachutes, weapons and war materiel for the Home Army (A.K.)," said Joe in a hushed voice.

"Oh, I hope nothing will happen to Bogdan," whispered the aunt, trembling with fear.

"Don't worry about anything now, Auntie! Our side has the upper hand now and the Germans are headed for defeat and are even afraid to show themselves at night! Bogdan will be home by morning!" Joe said feverishly.

"That's right, Auntie. Don't worry about Bogdan. He undoubtedly will be transporting these things that are being dropped down from the airplane and then will return soon," said Mary, trying to comfort the aunt.

The aunt calmed down a little and even some pride was entering her heart that her son was helping in work connected with the liberation of Poland. Despite everything, she was so enthusiastic about these most recent events that she didn't even think about sleep. She suggested, therefore, that Joe and Mary sit down on the bench near the doorway and wait with her for the return of Bogdan. Her suggestion was received with joy, as no one thought about sleep at such a moment. They all sat down on the long, wide bench and talked about what they had just seen as well as their plans for the future.

The aunt was just rising from the bench when Bogdan arrived. As usual, he jumped down from the wagon, unharnessed the horses, gave them water to drink, and led them into the stable. As he approached the group sitting outside the doorway, Joe was the first to speak:

"Bogdan, did you by any chance bring with you one of those American parachutes? Don't be afraid. Tell us about it. It is no longer a secret because we here saw everything. We thought for a minute that one of the packages would fall on our stable, but unfortunately the wind was blowing in another direction."

"I, too, saw the airplane and the parachutes, but I cannot say anything about that because we were sworn to secrecy. Don't ask me anything more about the matter because I will tell you nothing. Will you please get me some breakfast, Mother, because I am very hungry," said Bogdan.

"We understand very well, son; if it is a secret, then keep it secret. Wash yourself and say your prayers and I shall have breakfast ready for you. And when you have eaten, you may lie down and go to sleep because we won't be going out into the fields until this afternoon," decided the mother.

After breakfast, Joe and Mary went to their own room to take a short nap. Bogdan went to sleep in the hayloft. Frank led the cows out to pasture. The aunt busied herself indefatigably by doing chores out in the garden and preparing dinner.

And again in the home of Aunt Stepien, life passed peacefully. She worked in the fields with Bogdan during the day. Frank tended the cows in the pasture, happily whistling different tunes. Mary took care of Joe, who was able to get around on his own strength, although such activity tired him very much. Despite everything, he jokingly promised his aunt that soon he would leave with Bogdan to work in the fields. In the meantime, however, he was gaining strength with every passing day and his spare time was spent reading books which Frank borrowed from the local teacher.

One day, Joe's parents arrived to visit him and they brought some stupendous news. They said that "Bloody Eddy" had been seized and hanged by the partisans. It was in the village of Konary. "Eddy", as usual, was making expeditions into the area, always leaving behind him a trail covered with corpses. His last expedition into the area ended tragically for him. A group of partisans from the Peasants' Battalions (B.Ch.), learning that "Eddy was about to come into Konary, set up an ambush by the road leading from Klimontow to Konary. "Eddy", riding in the company of other men, was not even aware of what was happening when all of a sudden he was surrounded by a well-armed group of partisans. There was a short period of shooting, during which his companions were killed.

"Eddy" himself was taken alive by the partisans. On his person, he had many photographs taken of himself against the background of victims whom he had shot or hanged. He was pleading for his life because he feared death. The partisans interrogated him. He admitted all of his crimes, explained the photographs, and enumerated the various places where he had murdered innocent people. When all possible information was obtained from him, he was ordered to prepare for death. Then the partisans led him to a bent tree on which was hanging a halter. The one who had brought terror to the inhabitants of the entire Sandomierz District now walked to the place of his demise, trembling like a leaf in the wind. After a short pause, the death sentence was read and the criminal was executed. The justice of this world was satisfied; there remained only the satisfaction of divine justice.

The news about the death of "Bloody Eddy" was received favorably by Joe because it brought with it the opportunity for his return to his own home and to his beloved Jeziory. Until now, he never even thought about returning for fear of again meeting the murderer, who surely would not spare him. Now, however, the situation had changed.

Several weeks later, Joe returned to his home. He was completely well and able to get down from the wagon all by himself. The Adamczaks welcomed Joe and Mary with great joy and invited them to continue living in their home. Joe, however, decided to live elsewhere because he was afraid of encountering the Nazi police again. He and Mary took up their new residence in the village of Ruszcza. Both of them lived there to see the end of World War II and the total destruction of Hitlerism.

Shortly after the capitulation of Nazi Germany, Joe and Mary moved to Kowary, a lovely town in the Sudeten Mountains. There, Joe worked in a factory as an inspector of quality production and was very popular with the factory workers. From Kowary, Joe and Mary went to Blonie, near Warsaw, where Joe obtained a supervisory position in the ammunition factory. A few years after his retirement, Mary passed away. A lonely life of a widower was too oppressive for Joe so he remarried and the newly-married couple remained in Blonie near Warsaw. At the time of this writing (June 14, 1995), Joe is still living.

# Epilogue

As soon as I recovered somewhat from our exciting visit in Poland, I felt an urge to write about the highlights of our experiences for the benefit of my parishioners at St. Paul's Church in Weston, West Virginia. Since my wife, Mildred Juanita, wrote a sketchy diary every single day of our journey, I did not envision any problem in satisfying my literary urge. So I began to write, and my secretary, Judy Wood, typed what I had written for St. Paul's Sunday bulletins. Many of the parishioners who read, week after week, the account of our journey and the recollections of my personal experiences during World War II encouraged me to enlarge what I had written and publish it in book form. Since I trusted their judgment and took their encouragement seriously, I decided to work on this book.

My wife's diary provided me with the names of persons, locations, and the dates on which we visited them. My previous writings and the writings of my comrades-in-arms gave me the exact dates of the dramatic events which I have recollected in the first part of the book or have written in its second part.* In many of the dramatic events, described in both parts of the book, I took an active part or I witnessed them. In giving an account of these events, I made an effort to present them as truthfully as possible. My effort, however, does not exclude some inaccuracies or mistakes.

The names of the people and their pseudonyms are authentic. The same is true about the names of villages, towns, and cities. A good number of the individuals who took an active part in the dramatic events of World War II described in the

*My previous writings go all the way back to the fall of 1957, a few months after I left Poland and arrived in the United States. Among the writings of others are a number of letters written to me by Joe Mazgaj and his brother, Jan, in which they describe the events that constitute the core of my true story "He Is Still Alive".

book are still alive at the time of this writing (December 1995).*

Some of those who are no longer among the living died at the hands of Communists in Poland and in the former Soviet Union. Others could have lived up to the present time but their lives were shortened by inhuman tortures in Communist prisons.

After completing the writing of the essential parts of this book, I had a feeling of being reunited with my past life in Poland, from which I was uprooted and transplanted into the New World. The feeling of reunification with my early life gave me a new enthusiasm and energy in working on the final part of my World War II Memoirs, which I have been writing for a long time.

*Among those who are still living are: Stefan Franaszczuk ("Tarzan", "Orlicz"), Wlodzimierz Gruszczynski ("Jach"), Jan Osemlak ("Straceniec"), Janusz Szczerbatko ("Zygfryd"), Stanislaw Duma ("Topola"), Zbigniew Kabata ("Bobo"),, Arkadiusz Swiercz ("Iskra"), and Joe Mazgaj and his brother, Jan Mazgaj, both of whom are my first cousins.

# Index